NEW CENTURY BIBLE COMMENTARY

General Editors

RONALD E. CLEMENTS
(Old Testament)

MATTHEW BLACK
(New Testament)

The Song of Songs

THE NEW CENTURY BIBLE COMMENTARIES

EXODUS (J. P. Hyatt)
LEVITICUS AND NUMBERS (N. H. Snaith)*
DEUTERONOMY (A. D. H. Mayes)
JOSHUA, JUDGES, RUTH (John Gray)
1 AND 2 KINGS, Volumes 1 and 2 (Gwilym H. Jones)
1 AND 2 CHRONICLES (H. G. Williamson)
EZRA, NEHEMIAH, AND ESTHER (D. J. Clines)
JOB (H. H. Rowley)
PSALMS, Volumes 1 and 2 (A. A. Anderson)
ECCLESIASTES (R. N. Whybray)
THE SONG OF SONGS (John G. Snaith)
ISAIAH 1-39 (R. E. Clements)
ISAIAH 40-66 (R. N. Whybray)
JEREMIAH (Douglas Rawlinson Jones)
LAMENTATIONS (Iain W. Provan)
EZEKIEL (John W. Wevers)
HOSEA (G. I. Davies)
THE GOSPEL OF MATTHEW (David Hill)
THE GOSPEL OF MARK (Hugh Anderson)
THE GOSPEL OF LUKE (E. Earle Ellis)
THE GOSPEL OF JOHN (Barnabas Lindars)
THE ACTS OF THE APOSTLES (William Neil)
ROMANS, Second Edition (Matthew Black)
1 AND 2 CORINTHIANS (F. F. Bruce)
GALATIANS (Donald Guthrie)
EPHESIANS (C. Leslie Mitton)
PHILIPPIANS (Ralph P. Martin)
COLOSSIANS AND PHILEMON (Ralph P. Martin)
1 AND 2 THESSALONIANS (I. Howard Marshall)
PASTORAL EPISTLES (A. T. Hanson)
HEBREWS (R. McL. Wilson)
1 PETER (Ernest Best)
JAMES, JUDE, AND 2 PETER (E. M. Sidebottom)
JOHANNINE EPISTLES (K. Grayson)
THE BOOK OF REVELATION (G. R. Beasley-Murray)

* *Not yet available in paperback* *Other titles are in preparation*

NEW CENTURY BIBLE COMMENTARY

Based on the Revised Standard Version

THE SONG OF SONGS

JOHN G. SNAITH

Marshall Pickering
An Imprint of HarperCollins*Publishers*

WILLIAM B. EERDMANS PUBLISHING COMPANY, GRAND RAPIDS

Marshall Pickering is an Imprint of
HarperCollins*Religious*
Part of HarperCollins*Publishers*
77-85 Fulham Palace Road, London W6 8JB

First published 1993 in Great Britain by Marshall Pickering
and in the United States by Wm. B. Eerdmans Publishing Co.,
255 Jefferson Ave., S.E., Grand Rapids, Michigan 49503.

Printed in the United States of America
for Marshall Pickering and Wm. B. Eerdmans

1 3 5 7 9 10 8 6 4 2

A catalogue record for this book is
available from the British Library

Marshall Pickering ISBN 0-551-02629-4
Eerdmans ISBN 0-8028-0691-0

CONTENTS

PREFACE

This commentary appears as a contribution to the ongoing exegesis of the Song of Songs. The enormous size of the commentaries by L. Krinetzki, A. Robert/R. Tournay and M. H. Pope shows how restraint upon space in this volume has required me to select material from previous work. I have chosen to follow the more comprehensive work of G. Gerleman and W. Rudolph rather than the modern literary theories of M. Falk, the symbolic imagery of F. Landy and the feminist theology of A. Brenner. Happily M. V. Fox's commentary on the Song of Songs and the ancient Egyptian love lyrics appeared in 1985; this has enabled me to draw out more explicitly some of the Song's remarkably close parallels with the Egyptian material which had already been suggested by J. B. White and G. Gerleman.

As I learnt Hebrew as an Oxford undergraduate in 1955–7, I attended the late Sir Godfrey Driver's lectures on the Song of Songs. I still have my notes on those lectures and have included material from them where it is relevant. I refer to Driver's widely scattered articles and also draw upon many of his unpublished comments. As my knowledge of Hebrew received such encouragement from his pungent teaching and generous friendship, I am glad to dedicate this commentary to him – where it all started for me.

John G. Snaith
1991

ABBREVIATIONS

GENERAL

AB	*Anchor Bible*
AJSL	*American Journal of Semitic Languages and Literatures*
ANET	*Ancient Near Eastern Texts Relating to the Old Testament*, edited by J. B. Pritchard, 3rd edn., Princeton, 1969
BA	*Biblical Archaeologist*
CBQ	*Catholic Biblical Quarterly*
CIS	*Corpus Inscriptionum Semiticorum*
CPTOT	*Comparative Philology and the Text of the Old Testament*, J. Barr
DJD	*Discoveries in the Judaean Desert*
G-K	*Gesenius' Hebrew Grammar, as edited and enlarged by E. Kautzsch and revised by A. E. Cowley*, 2nd edn., London, 1910
GNB	*Good News Bible*, 1971
HEB	Hebrew
HUCA	*Hebrew Union College Annual*
JAOS	*Journal of the American Oriental Society*
JB	*Jerusalem Bible*, 1966
JBL	*Journal of Biblical Literature*
JSOT	*Journal for the Study of the Old Testament*
JQR	*Jewish Quarterly Review*
JSS	*Journal of Semitic Studies*
JTS	*Journal of Theological Studies*
K-B^3	*Hebräische und Aramäische Lexicon zum Alten Testament*, 3rd edn., 1990
LXX	*The Greek Septuagint Version*
MS, MSS	*manuscript(s)*
MT	*The Masoretic Text of the Old Testament*
NEB	*New English Bible*, 1970
NIV	*New International Version*, 1978

PEQ	*Palestine Exploration Quarterly*
Pesh.	Syriac Peshitta
RB	*Revue Biblique*
RSV	*Revised Standard Version*, 1952, 1973
Targ.	Aramaic Tarrum
VT	*Vetus Testamentum*
Vulg.	Latin Vulgate
ZAW	*Zeitschrift für die Alttestamentliche Wissenschaft*
ZDMG	*Zeitschrift der Deutschen Morgenländischen Gesellschaft*
ZDPV	*Zeitschrift des Deutschen Palästinavereins*

SELECT BIBLIOGRAPHY

COMMENTARIES *(cited in text by author's name only)*

G. L. Carr, *The Song of Solomon* (Tyndale Old Testament Commentaries), Leicester, 1984.

M. V. Fox, *The Song of Songs and Ancient Egyptian Love Songs*, Wisconsin, 1985.

W. J. Fuerst, *The Books of Ruth, Esther, Ecclesiastes, Song of Songs, Lamentations* (Cambridge Bible Commentaries), Cambridge, 1975.

G. Gerleman, *Ruth, das Hohelied* (Biblischer Kommentar), 2nd edn., Neukirchen, 1981.

R. Gordis, *The Song of Songs and Lamentations*, revised edn., New York, 1974.

M. D. Goulder, *The Song of Fourteen Songs* (JSOT supplement series 36), Sheffield, 1986.

P. Joüon, *Le Cantique des Cantiques*, Paris, 1909^2.

L. Krinetzki, *Das Hohelied: Kommentar zu Gestalt und Kerygma eines alttestamentlichen Liebeslied*, Düsseldorf, 1964.

O. Loretz, *Das alttestamentliche Liebeslied* (Alter Orient und Altes Testament 14), Neukirchen, 1971.

R. E. Murphy, *The Song of Songs* (Hermeneia Commentaries), Minneapolis, 1990 (appeared too late for use in this commentary).

M. H. Pope, *The Song of Songs* (Anchor Bible), New York, 1977.

H. Ringgren in H. Ringgren and A. Weiser, *Das Hohe Lied, Klagelieder, das Buch Esther: übersetzt und erklärt* (Das Alte Testament Deutsch), Göttingen, 1958.

A. Robert, R. Tournay and A. Feuillet, *Le Cantique des Cantiques*, Paris, 1963.

W. Rudolph, *Das Buch Ruth, Das Hohelied, Die Klagelieder* (Kommentar zum alten Testament), Gütersloh, 1962.

E. Würthwein in E. Würthwein, K. Galling and O. Plöger, *Die fünf Megilloth* (Handbuch zum alten Testament), Tübingen, 1969.

SPECIAL STUDIES *(cited in text by author's name only)*

J. Barr, *Comparative Philology and the Text of the Old Testament*, Oxford, 1968.

A. Brenner, *The Song of Songs* (Old Testament Guides), Sheffield, 1989.

M. Falk, *Love Lyrics from the Bible: a Translation and Literary Study of the Song of Songs*, Sheffield, 1982.

Y. Felics, *The Song of Songs: Nature, Epic and Allegory* (Hebrew), Jerusalem, 1964.

M. Landy, *Paradoxes of Paradise: Identity and Difference in the Song of Songs* (Almond Press), Sheffield, 1983.

D. Lys, *Le plus beau Chant de la Création: Commentaire du Cantique des Cantiques*, Paris, 1968.

J. B. White, *A Study of the Language of Love in the Song of Songs and ancient Egyptian Literature* (Scholars Press), Missoula, 1978.

ARTICLES

W. F. Albright, "Archaic Survivals in the Text of Canticles", *Hebrew and Semitic Studies presented to G. R. Driver*, ed. D. W. Thomas and W. D. McHardy, 1963, pp. 1–7.

J.-P. Audet, "Love and Marriage in the Old Testament", *Scripture* 10 (1958), pp. 79–83.

A. Bentzen, "Remarks on the Canonisation of the Song of Solomon", *Studia Orientalia Ioanni Pedersen, Studia Orientalia* 1 (1925), pp. 41–47.

A. Brenner, "Aromatics and Perfumes in the Song of Songs", *JSOT* 25 (1983), pp. 75–81.

G. R. Driver, "Supposed Arabisms in the Old Testament", *JBL* 55 (1936), pp. 101–20.

G. R. Driver, "Hebrew Notes on the Song of Songs and Lamentations" in W. Baumgartner et al. (eds.), *Festschrift für Alfred Bertholet zum 80 Geburtstag* (Tübingen), 1950, pp. 134–46.

G. R. Driver, "Lice in the Old Testament", *PEQ* 106 (1974), pp. 159–60.

M. V. Fox, "Scholia to Canticles (1:4 ba, 2:4, 14ba, 4:3, 6:12)", *VT* 33 (1983), pp. 199–206.

H. H. Hirschberg, "Some Additional Arabic Etymologies in Old Testament Lexicography", *VT* 11 (1961), pp. 373–85.

A. M. Honeyman, "Two Contributions to Canaanite Toponyms", *JTS* 50 (1949), pp. 50–52.

B. S. J. Isserlin, "Song of Songs IV, 4: an Archaeological Note", *PEQ* (1958), pp. 59–60.

R. E. Murphy, "Towards a Commentary on the Song of Songs", *CBQ* 39 (1977), pp. 482–96.

W. H. Shea, "The chiastic Structure of the Song of Songs", *ZAW* 92 (1980), pp. 378–96.

P. W. Skehan, "The Biblical Scrolls from Qumran and the Text of the Old Testament", *BA* 28 (1965), pp. 87–100.

J. G. Wetzstein, "Die syrische Dreschtafel", *Zeitschrift für Ethnologie* 5 (1873), pp. 270–302.

INTRODUCTION

to

The Song of Songs

A. CANONICAL STATUS, ALLEGORIZATION AND ORIGIN

In the Old Testament the Song of Songs appears among the Writings, the third division of the Hebrew canon. It is one of the *m^egillōṯ* or "scrolls", a group of five books which were read at major Jewish festivals. The Song itself was recited in the Passover liturgy – a usage which is hardly ancient, as it is not witnessed before the 8th century AD. Further, the Christian scholar Theodore of Mopsuestia (died c. 428 AD) considered the Song worthless because there was no public reading of it among Jews or Christians. The debate about the book's status goes right back to Rabbi Aqiba, who died in 135 AD. The Mishnah (*Yadaim* 3:5) records him as saying, "No man ever disputed about the Song of Songs that it does not render the hands unclean [i.e. profane hands become unclean through touching such a holy book], for all ages are not worth the day on which the Song of Songs was given to Israel: for all the Writings are holy, but the Song of Songs is the Holy of Holies." Rabbi Aqiba is also said (Tosefta, *Sanhedrin* 12:10) to have protested against profanation of the Song by singers who "trill their voices in chanting the Song of Songs in the banquet house and treat it as a sort of song" – a secular song, perhaps? Further, in the Meḥilta on Exod. 15:2 Aqiba is said to have related the young man in the Song to God and the maiden to Israel – so allegorization of the Song goes back as far as the 2nd century AD. Clearly, even at this early stage secular and religious (allegorical) interpretations were already doing battle with each other.

Traditionally the contents of the Old Testament canon were fixed by the Council of Jamnia, held c. 90 AD to consider whether certain books should be excluded. The above remarks from Rabbi Aqiba some years later show that the debate about the Song continued long after the Council. Although he himself saw it as a holy book, it is clear that some of his contemporaries viewed it as merely a good secular song or collection of songs. Both views were prevalent in Aqiba's day: the Song was sung as a pleasant ditty in pubs and expounded as an allegory of God's relationship with Israel. The allegorical view flourished in the Aramaic Targum, a very late Targum probably dating from the 6th century AD. This interpretation was followed by Christian scholars like Hippolytus of Rome (died in 235 AD) and has been adopted by many Catholic commentators in modern times.

However, the early importance of the allegorical interpretation should not be overstressed. R. Gordis, in tracing its history, claims openly that it was the reason for the Song's inclusion in the Canon. Certainly, the Song was later interpreted by Jews as an allegory of God's love for Israel and by Christians as an allegory of Christ's love for his Church. Clearly, in Aqiba's day both interpretations were current: the Targum and both Jewish and Christian medieval exegesis followed the allegorical path. But, since the discovery of many ancient Egyptian love songs and their translation by Michael Fox, many parallels and similarities of language and imagery between them and the biblical Song of Songs have been found. This suggests that there is every reason to suspect that the Song belonged to a particular genre of love lyrics in the ancient Near East – a genre which is now largely lost.

If the Song was originally a collection of love songs like the Egyptian ones – a view supported in this commentary – why was it read at Passover and thus included as one of the five *m^e^gillōṯ*? It is tempting to argue with Gordis that it was the allegorical interpretation that won the book its place in the canon. The first evidence of its use in the Passover liturgy comes from the 8th century AD, whereas the matter was hotly debated in Aqiba's day in the 2nd century, when it was asked not whether the Song should be included in the canon but whether it should *have been* included. There is even evidence for its use in pre-Christian times at Qumran, where four fragments are noted by P. W. Skehan (*BA* 28 (1965), p. 88). Perhaps traditions of Solomonic authorship led to canonical status: association with Solomon seems to have justified canonical status for both Proverbs and the questionable Ecclesiastes. Solomon's name is mentioned in the Song on five occasions apart from the title (1:5; 3:7, 9, 11; 8:11). Solomon was famed for literary activity and in 1 Kg. 4:32 is credited with "three thousand proverbs" and "a thousand and five" songs. However, we know from the apocryphal Wisdom of Solomon that it became traditional to ascribe to Solomon Jewish books of the wisdom type – and Wis. is indubitably late, written in Greek and full of derivative Greek philosophy. So attribution to Solomonic authorship seems likely. Considering his literary and amatory reputation, it seems not unreasonable to ascribe patronage or even authorship of this love poetry *par excellence* to the great lover, Solomon.

B. CONNEXIONS WITH FERTILITY CULTS?

But if canonization was due to neither allegorization nor Solomon's authorship, why *was* the Song included in the canon? Hosea (1–3) and Jeremiah (2:20–3:5) both speak of Yahweh and his people as bound by the covenant, and they use marital faithfulness as an image of loyalty to God. But in the Song there is no such explicit theological connexion. The Targum (allegorically) related the kissing in 1:2 to the giving of the law, suggesting a link between the earliest part of the book and the Exodus and the passover, but again there is nothing explicit. (For further examples of allegorical interpretation see the Afterword following the commentary.) A. Bentzen (in *Festschrift für J. Pedersen*, pp. 41–7) thought that the custom of reading the Song at Passover arose through association with the time of year, as Passover was celebrated in the spring and the Song is full of spring imagery. Usage at Passover in synagogue worship was then rationalized and given a base more theological than just the time of year.

But the Song is unashamedly sexual, and not apparently religious at all. It is also quite free of any specific references to the fertility cults of Israel's neighbours. Since no cultic-mythological significance is apparent, we should acknowledge the Song's free and open attitude to human sexuality as opposed to the sexual religious practices of Canaanite fertility religion. Perhaps the Song was included in the canon because it was a non-mythological, non-cultic, non-idolatrous, outright, open celebration of God-given sexual love. We may recognize the Song's worth in this respect and value it because it is uncorrupted by idolatrous fertility religions – but do these considerations alone explain its inclusion in the canon? It may help to remember that, unlike Christianity, orthodox Jewry has rarely been prudish in sexual matters. Yet, even so, later Jews and Christians tried to suppress the Song's explicit sensuousness by allegorizing every detail in terms of God's dealings with his people. Hosea had presented God's relations with Israel in terms of courtship and marriage: the Song only takes this approach further.

C. LITERARY STRUCTURE

It is fairly evident that the Song of Songs consists of a collection of short poems strung together. Often it is clear where the speakers change – indeed, some scholars have detected in the book a dramatic dialogue. Sometimes the divisions between the poems are indicated by a clear change in the gender of the speaker (cf. 2:1, 8; 5:10; 6:4): such changes are more obvious in the original text because Hebrew distinguishes form of gender more than English. Some individual poems close with an adjuration to the daughters of Jerusalem (cf. 2:7; 3:5; 5:8; 8:4); once (anomalously) the daughters of Zion are addressed (3:11). Both groups seem to act as choruses rather like those in Greek classical drama. Occasionally this chorus is not named: a verse, spoken in the first person plural, appears and concludes a defined section (1:4; 6:1, 13). Occasionally such a remark from the chorus serves to link two poems: in 5:9 the daughters of Jerusalem, addressed in the previous verse, ask a question which leads into a new poem describing the handsomeness of the young man. In 1:8 an anonymous third party (the chorus? the author?) provides a similar link verse. Sometimes a poem's boundary is marked by a decisive change in subject-matter (cf. 2:1, 17); sometimes the literary device known as inclusion marks the beginning and the end of a poem (cf. 4:1 and 7; 5:9 and 16). 6:1–3 forms a discrete poem comprising the chorus' question (v. 1) and the beloved's answer (vv. 2–3).

The boundaries of some individual units are much less clear: for example, the *waṣf*s or admiration songs in 6:4–7 and 8–10 are less fulsome and more fragmentary than those in 5:10–16 and

7:1–5. The short poem in 6:11–13 is difficult to understand as a whole due to the problems raised by the "dance before two armies" (v. 13) and the girl's "fancy" putting her in a "chariot" beside her "prince" (v. 12) (on both see the commentary). Some passages defy division into separate units (cf. 4:8–5:1), and towards the end of the book the poems become more fragmentary – see, for example, the very uneven song of admiration in 7:6–9. Further, the divisions between separate poems in chapter 8 are much debated by commentators, as shown in the commentary. However, the overall pattern of the Song remains fairly clear – that is, a loose collection or concatenation of poems which are often concluded by comments from a chorus (the daughters of Jerusalem).

This view receives support from the Egyptian love lyrics published by M. V. Fox. As I have said in the Preface, Fox's work has shown how close these Hebrew songs are to the Egyptian lyrics – in spite of the huge gap in time (probably at least 800 years) separating the two groups. There are very many similarities in imagery, wording and general atmosphere, some of which will be illustrated in this commentary. The large time gap makes it foolish to suggest that the Egyptian songs had any direct influence on the Song of Songs, but the large amount of similarity does show that the genre of short love lyrics probably persisted and developed during this period in the Near East – and there are Mesopotamian parallels too. Of such poems most have perished; those published by Fox have survived through burial in the sands of Egypt and just happen to have been discovered. The Song of Songs was preserved because it was used liturgically – although before that, according to Rabbi Aqiba, it was enjoyed as a collection of really good, probably secular, love songs. So we may confidently assert that there was a whole genre of this type of poetry spanning centuries, examples of which survive in the Egyptian lyrics and the biblical Song of Songs.

But, if the Song of Songs is a collection of individual songs, wherein lies the book's unity? M. Goulder accepted it as a "semi-continuous sequence" of songs, but claimed that the songs moved "in a progression from the arrival of the princess at Solomon's court to her acknowledgement by the King as his favourite queen". Such dramatic unity seems to me difficult to sustain: it is much more natural to see a rather looser collection of songs on the Egyptian pattern. However, the Song is by no means a random collection: there is a common imagery and a certain cohesiveness throughout, the characters of lover and beloved remain surprisingly consistent, and there are a remarkable number of repetitive phrases which serve as refrains and hold the whole together. These repetitions or repetends (Fox), together with the recurrent imagery of animals, flowers and the like, make the songs in the biblical book much more uniform than those in the Egyptian collection. Amid the imagery and behind the diversity there is enough progression to suggest to Goulder that a single dramatic plot underlies the whole – but the book remains more a well edited, carefully arranged sequence of poems than a real drama. The Song takes a romance between two characters, holds it up and looks at it from various different viewpoints, using the lyric imagery which is to hand. The romance includes wishful thinking, lonely misery, vivid dreams and happy companionship. The Egyptian parallels help us to appreciate the background, which would otherwise have been largely lost; but the (unknown) author of the Song has composed or arranged poems from that background to illustrate many different forms of human love.

D. AUTHORSHIP AND DATE

What, then, of the Song's authorship? Solomonic authorship is probably a literary fiction, as in Proverbs and the Wisdom of Solomon. The Egyptian songs suggest that the Song is a collection of love songs of the same type. If, then, the editor picked out and collected together various songs from an existing stock of love songs and then skilfully blended them into this loosely strung unity, it is strange that songs with such conveniently close phraseology were available – unless there was (as one might suspect) a truly large body of songs to choose from – all unknown to us now. The link passages were undoubtedly supplied by the editor, but there is sufficient variety in the character of the longer songs (especially the *waṣf*s) to make it unlikely that he composed the whole as a kind of song cycle. Some of the songs he may have selected from the stock available, whereas others he may have composed himself – we cannot tell, nor does it matter a great deal. As with other biblical books, it is the finished product that we handle and interpret. I therefore suggest multiple authorship for the songs with a single, overall editor.

This makes the question of the date of the Song's composition unclear, partly because many of the constituent songs may have existed for a long time before the collection, and partly because we have very little biblical Hebrew poetry of the same type with which to compare the Song. References to Solomon are irrelevant because of the fictional character he frequently assumes in the Old Testament. Mention of Tirzah (6:4), the capital of the northern kingdom before Samaria became the capital during Omri's reign in c. 870 BC, need not mean an earlier date than that, as the earlier capital would not have been forgotten. It is mentioned in order to create a play on words to enhance the girl's beauty (see commentary). Linguistic evidence is uncertain, due to the lack of surviving poetry of a similar type: words and constructions we may cite as late may well have been used in Hebrew lyric poetry which is now lost. Several seemingly late words and constructions are used: the passive participle used in an active sense in *ʾaḥūzēy ḥereḇ*, "girt with swords", in 3:8; the use of the relative *še-* in place of *ʾašer* (though the earlier Phoenician used *ʾeš*); the absence of the *waw* consecutive form of verbs. Various nouns of later origin appear: *kōṯel*, "wall", in 2:9; *pardēs*, "orchard", in 4:13; *beroṯîm*, "cedars", in 1:17.

The linguistic evidence suggests that the Song was composed in its present state late in the history of the biblical, classical language, but early enough to have gained acceptance as a religious book. Indeed, the fact that a fragment of the Song has been found at Qumran suggests that the book must have been included in the library there (*DJD* III, pp. 112–14). But although a late date must be given to the final collection, its individual constituent parts need not be so dated. Indeed, their telling likeness to the earlier Egyptian songs suggests that some of them may be very early indeed, unless the lyric tradition in Israel lasted all through the centuries from those early times unknown to us.

E. ANALYSIS OF THE TEXT

1:1	The Heading
1:2–4	The girl's desire for her partner
1:5–8	The girl's embarrassment
1:9–17	Compliments exchanged
2:1–7	Heightening compliments
2:8–17	The lover shut out
3:1–5	A happy dream
3:6–11	A royal wedding?
4:1–7	Admiration of the beloved
4:8–5:1	Away to the delights of love!
5:2–8	Another nocturnal search
5:9	A link verse
5:10–16	Admiration of the lover
6:1–3	Another link passage
6:4–7	Less fulsome admiration
6:8–10	The incomparable one
6:11–13	Another link passage
7:1–5	Renewed admiration of the beloved
7:6–9	A fragmentary poem of admiration
7:10–13	A country walk for lovers
8:1–4	Back to mother's house
8:5	A fragment – or two?
8:6–7	The power of love
8:8–10	A dialogue of playful banter
8:11–12	Two different vineyards
8:13–14	A closing invitation

THE SONG OF SONGS

THE HEADING
1:1

1:1. The Song of Songs, which is Solomon's: This is clearly a title placed at the head of the book. The phrase, **The Song of Songs** (*šîr haššîrîm*) does not imply that the book is a collection of songs (though it may be this – see the Introduction on the composition of the book), but illustrates one way of expressing the superlative in Hebrew. The construction is used, elsewhere in the OT – for example, in Ec. 1:2, *heḇel hᵉḇālîm*, "vanity of vanities" (*RSV*) or "the most absurd absurdity" (Fox). It is also used of the innermost shrine in the temple: *qᵉḏōš haqqᵉḏōšîm*, "the holiest place", i.e. the Holy of Holies. When Rabbi Aqiba was defending the Song's inclusion in the canon, he used this construction in a clever play on words: "all writings [sc. in the OT, his Bible] are holy, but the Song of Songs is holy of holies" or "holiest of all". The relative pronoun (*ᵃšer*) used in **which is Solomon's** appears only here in the Song, even though this is the usual form in biblical Heb. Elsewhere in the book, in poetic passages, *še-* is used; this is the relative pronoun regularly used in post-biblical and modern Hebrew. Some have claimed that this use of *še-* shows that the poem is late in date. However, Phoenician inscriptions early in the OT period use *š* or *'š* (we don't know the vowels in Phoenician) regularly as the relative pronoun, and *še-* appears also in the very early Song of Deborah in Jg. 5, which displays several early northern features. So this usage does not indicate a late date. The *NEB* translators, noting that *ᵃšer* does not fit the style of the Song, revocalized the consonants as *'āšîr*, "I will sing (the song of all songs to Solomon)". But this is unnecessary: it is no surprise that the prose heading, which was probably added later, should differ in style from the poetry.

That **which is Solomon's** is intended to ascribe authorship to Solomon is uncertain. The preposition used here (*lᵉ*) is also used in headings to Ugaritic poems to mean "concerning" a particular deity, and *lᵉḏavid* is used in the titles of psalms, attaching them loosely to the general patronage of David. As I noted in the Introduction, so many features of the Song can be linked with the traditional picture of Solomon that it is no surprise to see his name attached to the book, although H. H. Hirschberg considers Solomon the author to be an entirely different person from the famous king (*VT* 11 (1961), p. 380). But whether the preposition indicates authorship or subject-matter of the poems remains uncertain.

THE GIRL'S DESIRE FOR HER PARTNER
1:2–4

The first unit of the Song describes the girl's passionate yearning for her lover's presence. This lyric genre appears again in 2:4–5, 10–13 and 8:6, and is found frequently in Egyptian love poetry (cf. White, p. 152; Fox, pp. 16–17 and *passim*).

2. O that you would kiss me with the kisses of your mouth: *RSV* here changes the subject pronoun of the Heb. verb. The Heb. reads, "Let *him* kiss me with the kisses of *his* mouth", then changing to the second person singular, **For your love is better than wine**. *RSV* thus tries to make the translation consistent with English usage. J.-P. Audet (*Scripture* 10 (1958), pp. 79–83) argues that the first part of this verse (**O that you . . . kisses of your mouth**) represents the original title given to a pre-exilic song (both words and melody) – a title now prefaced by a further title (i.e. v. 1) given to the whole collection by the final, post-exilic editor. But such shifts of person were not uncommon in poetry: cf. Dt. 32:15; Jer. 22:24; Mic. 7:19; Ps. 23:1–3, 4–5 (in none of these does the *RSV* "correct" the text as here). This shift of pronoun, called *enallage*, is surprising, but the ancient versions show the same variations, so the text is probably correct.

Wordplay may be seen in the juxtaposition of *yiššāqēnī* ("let him kiss me") and *minn*ᵉ*šîqōṯ* ("with the kisses of"), both derived from the root *nšq*, meaning "kissed". As L. Krinetzki notes, we can appreciate onomatopoeic sounds of kissing in the Heb. words. Some have detected a pun, reading the same consonants with different vowels: *yašqēnī*, a hiphil causative tense from *šqh*, "drank". Fox suggests a hidden pun between "drank" and "kissed", which G. R. Driver expressed well as "let him drench me (with kisses)".

with the kisses of your mouth is not superfluous: nose kisses were common in the ancient Near East, and the author, by stressing the mouth, emphasizes that the girl is requesting that more intimate kind of kiss. **with** translates the Heb. *min* ("from" or "from among"), which is frequently used in a partitive sense: "some of". Some commentators have even debated the number of kisses implied here, but that is idle speculation.

For your love is better than wine: better translates the Heb. *ṭôḇ*, which may rather have the same sense as the Ugaritic *ṭb* used of wine, whence Pope's "sweeter than wine".

3. your anointing oils are fragrant: more literally, "as for scent, your oils are good" (Fox). Fox's translation makes the construction clear: the preposition before "scent" in the Heb. (*lᵉ*) could introduce *casus pendens*, as Fox's translation suggests (*G-K* §143e), but it may also echo an emphatic particle used in Assyrian and Arabic. G. R. Driver (*Festschrift für Alfred Bertholet*, p. 134) understood this prefix as "surely" (cf. also F. Nötscher, "Zum emphatischen Lamedh", *VT* 3 (1953), p. 379). In **your name is oil poured out** the English loses the paronomasia in Heb. between *šemen* ("oil") and *šᵉmeḵa* ("your name"). A **name** represents the real self, not just a person's reputation. **oil poured out** represents *šemen tûrāq* in the Heb. *Tûrāq* is usually taken as a passive verbal form (hophal imperfect) from *ryq*, "was empty", linked to "oil" in a relative clause without the relative pronoun being expressed. Such abbreviated constructions were certainly used in poetry, but unfortunately here the genders don't agree: *tûrāq* is a feminine verbal form, and *šemen*, a masculine noun, cannot be the subject of a feminine verb. One scholar has delightfully suggested that "grammatical accuracy was overlooked by the maiden in her ardour"! One Ugaritic text cites *trqm* in a list of wines and oils. Some commentators take *tûrāq* as the proper name of some specially luxurious oil ("Oil of Turaq" – Fox): this is probably the nearest we can get to a solution. Pouring oil indicated wealth in those days, but to our modern minds it seems a strange thing to do!

4. Draw me after you: probably the girl is merely saying to her lover, "Take me along with you." But, as W. Rudolph notes, the accents in the Heb. text divide the construction differently, linking the prepositional phrase **after you** with the second verb, **let us make haste**: "Draw me, let us hurry after you." This is strange. In the first words of this verse, as in v.3, the girl addresses her lover in the second person: she speaks of **us** hurrying after **you**. If this first person represents herself and her lover, as seems natural, then who does **you** refer to? *Enallage* accounts for change of person in the verbal form, but here an additional character seems to appear. The Targum, allegorizing hard, interprets **us** as the Israelites hastening after God, and Rudolph detects this allegorizing tendency even in the editing of the Masoretes. Both **we** and **us** refer to the Israelites: **we** would then be a collective personification, **us** a reference to individuals – almost an interpretative gloss for pietistic reasons. The first persons fit vv. 2 and 3, but problems arise with the change of person in the next phrase, **The king has brought me into his chambers**. This is more than *enallage*, mere change of persons; a third character, **The king**, seems to be introduced.

Traditionally **The king** was identified with Solomon, but more recent commentators have identified the term as a title for a bridegroom, thus making this part of the Song a wedding celebration. This interpretation was much strengthened by J. J. Wetzstein, a German consul in Syria in the 19th century, who claimed that there was in Syria a wedding custom in which bride and groom were crowned on a threshing platform and hailed as king and queen "as in the Song of Solomon". Such customs certainly live long in popular lore, and bridegrooms are often called kings in Arabic poetry; but the time gaps are long and too much has been read into this custom. As Fox writes, "the lovers are called kings, princes and queens because of the way love makes them feel about each other and about themselves". In support he cites very similar nomenclature in ancient Egyptian love songs.

Both Septuagint and Vulgate fell to the temptation to read eroticism into the text: for **your love** (*dōḏeyḵā*) they translated "your breasts" (*daddeyḵā*). The two words were indistinguishable in unvocalized Heb. script.

In **rightly do they love you** the Heb. for **rightly** (*mēyšārîm*) is problematical, and the ancient translations take it variously.

Fox may well be correct in detaching **more than wine** (*miyyayin*) from the previous phrase and revocalizing it as a construct (*miyyēyn*), thus translating the last phrase in the verse, "more than smooth wine do they love you".

THE GIRL'S EMBARRASSMENT
1:5–8

In the previous unit the girl expressed her ardent longing for her beloved in exultant terms, using a royal travesty. Now the mood changes to modesty – it seems somewhat excessive, but such feelings are common in matters of love. Like Cinderella, the girl sees herself as lowly and quite unworthy of her beloved. The Cinderella motif preceded that folktale by many centuries – it is indeed an eternal situation. This unit uses a different travesty, that of the garden and the gardener: the grand atmosphere of things royal is exchanged for the servitude of the vineyard-keeper. No longer does the king bring the girl into his chambers: rather she wanders alone, desperately searching among shepherds in the open grassland. She addresses the daughters of Jerusalem in v. 5 as a sympathetic third party, as in 2:7; 3:5; 5:8, 16 (in 3:11 she addresses the daughters of Zion). Whether it is they or the young lover who reply to her in v. 8 is uncertain – scholars disagree – but certainly this unit forms a dialogue with v. 8 as an answer to the girl's misgivings.

5. I am very dark, but comely: The Heb. particle *w*^e^ between the two adjectives often means simply *and*, but sometimes it has an adversative force, as in *RSV* here. The adversative force of the Heb. has led some to see colour prejudice here (cf. Pope's discussion of blackness and melanophobia in Jewish and Christian exegesis, pp. 308–18). It is surely quite wrong to import into the text modern racial and colour problems. The girl's dark colour is adequately explained in v. 6: she has been excessively sunburnt while working in a vineyard in the heat of the day. So, as M. D. Goulder says, the text does not imply that she is a negress. However, it certainly does imply that her colour is disapproved of. This contrast is made clearer by the address to the **daughters of**

Jerusalem, city ladies whose skin is presumably well kept and preserved from strong sunlight. **the tents of Kedar: Kedar** sounds like the Heb. *qāḏar*, "was black". Mention of **Kedar** is thus linked with **very dark** by paronomasia in the Heb. The place **Kedar** is mentioned in Jer. 49:28 in parallel to "the people of the East". The Assyrian king Assurbanipal is said to have conquered a king of *ki-da-ri* or *ki-di-ri* in his campaigns against the Arabs (*ANET*, pp. 298f.). **the curtains of Solomon:** the Heb. *y^e^rî'āh* is used of both tents and curtains, especially in the Pentateuch. It is also the word for the costly fabrics used for the hangings in Solomon's temple. However, several modern translations have "Shalmah" or "Salmah" for **Solomon** here: thus *NEB*, "the tent curtains of Shalmah". The curtains of Solomon's temple certainly seem an odd poetic parallel to Kēdar, a desert Bedouin tribe, and there is a continual tendency in the OT for the renowned Solomon to creep into appropriate settings, and here a king was mentioned in the previous verse. Pliny (*Nat. Hist.* VI 26.118) mentions the *Salmāni*, a tribe in the Syrian/Arabian desert near Babylon, and a Nabataean inscription (*CIS* II/I no. 197) mentions the *slmw*, a tribe said to have preceded the Nabataeans at Petra. To compare the girl's swarthy skin to swarthy Bedouin tentcloth suits this context better than Solomon's rich hangings.

6. because the sun has scorched me: The Heb. word used here (*šāzap*) occurs elsewhere only in Job 20:9 and 28:7, meaning "looked in" (so LXX here). Plainly it makes no sense to stop people looking at a girl because the sun has "looked in" on her! So *RSV* has taken the verb as an Aramaic form of the Heb. *šāḏap̄*, "scorched". M. Dahood (*Biblica* 45 (1964), pp. 406f.) even saw here a verb derived from *zep̄eṯ*, "pitch", meaning "made black as pitch". **My mother's sons:** Lys claimed that this phrase was used in polygamous societies to distinguish half-brothers from real brothers, who would often stand for their sisters in marriage (cf. Gen. 24:29ff.; 34:13ff.). **were angry with me:** Probably from *nḥr*, cf. Accadian *naḫāru*, "to rage" or "to snort" (G. R. Driver, *JTS* 34 (1933), pp. 380f., cf. LXX and Vulg. "fought"), rather than a wrongly vocalized niphal of *ḥārāh*, "was angry". **they made me keeper of the vineyards** fits well the allegorical kind of interpretation followed by the Targum: Israel was the keeper of

God's will/law in the world. However, this phrase has more in common with the bucolic atmosphere of the Egyptian love lyrics, where similar imagery occurs. **my own vineyard** is probably a symbol for the beloved's own person – not that she has given her charms to others, but she has not taken care of herself in her open-air work. In this verse three times we find the relative *šĕ-* discussed in 1:1.

7. you whom my soul loves: There is no platonic dualism here between soul and body. The Heb. *nepeš*, here translated **soul**, refers to the whole person. If we were to pick any bodily organ for this word, it would be "my heart" (*JB*), but "my true love" (*NEB*) gives the sense well. Presumably **noon** was the time when a shephered would rest in any shade that was available. **like one that wanders** represents a change in the Heb. text. For MT *keʿōṭyāh RSV* reads *keṭōʿiyyāh* as the strong form (*G-K* §75v) of the qal active participle feminine singular of *ṭaʿah*, "wandered" (cf. Vulg. *vagari*, also Pesh.). This suits well the girl's wandering in the open in the previous verses. MT seems to have the present qal participle of *ʿāṭāh*, "wrapped oneself" (so LXX; cf. *RSV* mg.). Prostitutes wrapped themselves closely in clothes, as does Tamar in Gen. 38:14 to trick Judah into having intercourse with her. But if the girl is here seeking her beloved, whom she knows, there is no need for her to dress up like a prostitute. This may explain why in Vulg. Jerome assumed metathesis of two letters and translated "wandered". However, G. R. Driver (*PEQ* 106 (1974), pp. 159f.) quoted K. Galling (*ZAW* 24 (1904), pp. 119–21) claimed that it was customary in the ancient Orient for girls to delouse the head of their beloved and that many examples of this exist in Arabic literature, where the Arabic verb *ʿaṭa* is used. In Jer. 43:12 LXX translates the Heb. *yaʿaṭeh* as "pick lice (off one's garment)". This suggests that the translators of LXX knew a meaning for the Heb. root which is preserved now only in Arabic. *NEB* translates here: "that I may not be left picking lice (as I sit among your companions' herds)". Certainly, if the girl had become so dark through exposure to the sun she has hardly been veiled as a prostitute: delousing may therefore be preferable to veiling.

8. The maiden's uncertainty is now answered, but not very helpfully. There is no answer to her question of v. 7, but rather mocking encouragement to go out and look for her lover. The verse forms a link with the next unit, where the speaker changes to the man. This link function is often performed by the daughters of Jerusalem, but they are not mentioned here, and the comment seems too caustic for their habitual position as a kind of Greek chorus. G. Gerleman suggested that the poet himself was speaking – comment by the poet would account well for the distance from events here assumed.

COMPLIMENTS EXCHANGED
1:9–17

This rather longer unit contains a dialogue of mutual admiration between the girl and her lover, possibly with a third party looking on. The lovers express their feelings for each other in brief *waṣf*-like poems (in German known as *Beschreibungsliede*, songs which describe the beauty of the loved one feature by feature). The imagery is varied, and has been thought to indicate three separate poems: vv. 9–11, 12–14 and 15–17. But it seems unnecessary to separate them entirely, and we probably have one single unit with three sections each containing six carefully balanced lines. Images are drawn mainly from nature (animals and the like), precious stones and scents – all images notably paralleled in the Egyptian songs. The royal fiction of v. 4 reappears in v. 12. The rustic fiction of vv. 6 and 7 also appears again: the couple lie under the trees (v. 17), just as the girl wandered among the flocks earlier (v. 7). The lover speaks in vv. 9–10, the girl in vv. 12–14; they make brief replies – the lover in v. 15 and the girl in vv. 16–17. V. 11 falls outside this pattern, as the first person plural **We** shows. The content of this verse is very similar to that of v. 8, where the author seemed to insert his own thoughts. If the same happens here, then we may assume that the author is using the first person plural of himself or identifying himself with the daughters of Jerusalem. As in v. 8, he uses the device of a third party to comment on the situation.

9. First the lover compares his girl to **a mare of Pharaoh's**

chariots. The MT is difficult, reading *sûsāṯî*, "my mare" with the first person singular suffix, a reading confirmed by the translations in the ancient versions. However, the ending *-î* is not necessarily a personal suffix, but possibly a vocalic link between closely related nouns known as the *ḥireq compaginis* (cf. *G-K* §90k-n). G. R. Driver and Pope have claimed that in Egypt chariots were drawn in civil life by two horses and in war by one horse only. In a battle a single mare running loose could cause havoc among otherwise reliable stallions. This actually happened at the battle of Kadesh in the reign of Pharaoh Thutmosis III. Thus *NEB* reads the plural *l^{e}sûsôṯ*, "to (Pharaoh's) chariot horses". This mention of horses has nothing to do with sexual arousal (*pace* Pope) but rather conveys the idea of ornamental beauty – Egyptians frequently adorned their horses with decorated bridles and harnesses.

Some of these poetic comparisons seem strange to us today. They refer not to feelings or qualities but to material, impersonal things. For example, in 4:4 the girl's neck is said to be **like the tower of David, built for an arsenal**; its **thousand bucklers** are probably an image for the many necklaces she is wearing. This metaphor is strange, even abhorrent, to us. We must recognize that different cultures see beauty in different things.

Horses were prized possessions in Egypt, and papyri show that the Egyptians also felt strong affection towards their steeds. Solomon imported horses from Egypt (1 Kings 10:26–29). The mention of **Pharaoh** here provides another link between these Israelite love songs and a traditional poetic form in Egypt.

10. The different items in vv. 10 and 11 are sometimes difficult to identify, but there is no excuse for LXX and Vulg. taking the Heb. *tôrîm* as "doves". Not even the ancients could have adorned their cheeks with doves! Jerome shows signs of making the best of a bad job: Vulg. reads *pulchrae sunt genae tuae sicut turturis*, "your cheeks are beautiful as those of doves". But are doves' cheeks beautiful? These translations confused two Heb. homonyms: *tôr*, "dove", and *tôr*, "plait" or "turn", possibly of hair. The best translation here is probably "bangles" rather than **ornaments**, which is altogether too general. In Egyptian art we sometimes see women wearing circular or semi-circular ornaments (perhaps ear-rings) which hang down and partially hide the cheeks. The Heb. word for **strings of jewels**, *ḥ^{a}rūzîm*, is related to the Arabic noun *ḥarazu(n)*, "beads strung together" or "a neck-ornament", which suits this context well.

11. This verse intensifies the effect of v. 10. Now it is not just ornaments and pearls, but **gold** and **silver**. The Heb. word for **ornaments** is the same as that used in v. 10 – it is probably repeated quite deliberately to intensify the effect. As Fox suggests, the meaning may be: as her cheeks look so lovely in bangles, we'll go further and give her golden bangles! The decoration of v. 10 is thus not replaced but doubled in richness. The word *n^{e}quddôṯ* used for **studded** is a noun ("studs") related to the word used in Gen. 30:32 (*nāqōḏ*) for "speckled" sheep and goats. Thus this added decoration is probably silver overlaid on the golden surface of the bangles just described. "Beads" (*NEB*) and "kinks" (Goulder) seem inadequate, but **studded** seems just right.

12. The speaker is now the girl, who talks of her lover in terms of the royal fiction in 1:4. The image of sweet smells, frequent in Egyptian love poetry and used in 1:3 of oil, reappears here. The sweet scent of the girl attracts the man to her as he relaxes.

The Heb. for **on his couch** (*bim^{e}sibbô*) has caused difficulty, which is increased by the lack of any verb in the temporal clause (though the verb "to be" is often left to be supplied in this way). The same root appears frequently in an adverb meaning "round about" (*sāḇîḇ*), and the noun (*mēsāḇ*), here with a pronominal suffix, is used in the plural in 2 Kg. 23:5 of the suburbs of ("places round about") Jerusalem. In Job 37:12 the plural seems to denote the different directions of the moving clouds and in Ec. 1:6 the circuits of wind currents. The adverb *sāḇîḇ* is frequently prefixed by the preposition *l^e*, meaning "around". But, if this were the meaning here, the verse would then become nonsensical: "While the king was in his own vicinity [i.e. *bim^{e}sibbô*, 'round about himself'], my nard gave forth its fragrance." Thus some scholars suggest that the original text should read *bim^{e}sibbî*, "around me" or "near me": the girl smells delightful while she is near him. This reading makes good sense. But the first-person suffix is not recognized by the ancient translations, although the difference in Heb. script between *-ô* ("his") and *-î* ("my") is very slight. It is better to recognize here an early occurrence of the later Mishnaic noun *m^esibbāh*, "couch", as in *RSV*. That a king should summon a girl while he is lying on his couch fits the royal fiction well, as shown in the book of Esther (cf. especially Est. 4:11).

nard, an expensive fragrant ointment imported from India, was used frequently in the Mediterranean world as a love-charm: see J. P. Brown in *VT* 19 (1969), pp. 160–64, where examples are cited from classical poetry, from Alcaeus and Horace, and from nard's native India. Nard was considered to possess aphrodisiac qualities. Origen claimed that spikenard gave scent only when its hairy stem was rubbed or squeezed.

13. The Heb. word for **bag** (*ṣ^erōr*) indicates a small sachet in which money and precious objects could be kept for safety (cf. Gen. 42:35; Hag. 1:6). The word was also used figuratively for the custody of precious things (cf. Job's transgressions "sealed up in a bag" in Job 14:17). The Mishnah (Shabbath 6:3) refers to such a "spice-box".

The word **myrrh** (*mōr*) is probably related to the adjective *mār*, "bitter". Myrrh was an aromatic gum or resin imported from South Arabia or Africa. Well known in Assyrian, Babylonian and Ugaritic texts, it is frequently referred to in Egyptian love poetry. While a man was away from home, his wife would sometimes perfume her bed with myrrh for her lover (Prov. 7:17–19): thus it was an aphrodisiac. The *RSV*'s translation of *yālîn* as **lies** primly avoids the issue: the verb *lîn* means "spend the night", and often means more than one night (cf. modern Heb. *mālōn*, "hotel"). So really this verse is saying that the lover is spending the night **between** the girl's **breasts**. The aphrodisiac associations of myrrh serve to emphasize the erotic implications even more.

14. The girl may seem to change the sexual metaphor when she calls her lover **a cluster of henna blossoms**. Henna flowers in June and, like other plants mentioned in the Song, gives off a strong, sweet scent. This scent was much used in the ancient world – Gerleman notes that Nubian women used it to mask the smell of goats! In Ugaritic texts the scent of henna heralds the approach of the goddess Anath. But more than aromatic imagery seems to be indicated here: it is not the colour of henna flowers (yellow) which is significant but their shape. The Heb. word for

cluster (*'eškōl*) is used frequently of the shape of a bunch of grapes: a long, thickish cluster tapering slightly to the bottom. Y. Felics (p. 48) provides a drawing of henna fruit and blossom: the fruit are little round berries (whence *'eškōl* is used also of grapes), but the blossom forms in tapering panicles rather like lilac flowers. Thus **a cluster of henna flowers** is in shape not unlike the human male sexual organ when extended: one scholar has even suggested "spike" as a suitable translation! Indeed, it is difficult to see what else the phrase can mean on the lips of the girl as she is describing her young man. The previous verse refers to the female breasts, and this verse balances it with a delicate image of the male sexual organ.

En-gedi is an oasis on the western shore of the Dead Sea at the exit of a well-watered green valley. Its luxuriant vegetation stands out against the surrounding extremely arid, barren desert, and its fresh running water differs greatly from the salty, viscous fluid in the Dead Sea. En-gedi has thus been famous for its vines and streams ever since antiquity: Ben Sira (Sir. 24:14), Josephus (Ant. IX. 1, 2) and Pliny (*Nat. Hist.* XII 14.24) all refer to its rich fertility.

15. In the last three verses of the chapter the dialogue between the lovers intensifies with a rapid exchange of compliments. The man's opening words in this verse, **Behold, you are beautiful, my love** are echoed almost exactly in the girl's words in v. 16: **Behold, you are beautiful, my beloved**. The two compliments differ only in the words of address used and, of course, in the masculine and feminine genders in the Heb., which are not reflected in the English translation. Such repetition emphasizes the lovers' mutual satisfaction in each other's presence. The *wasf*-like atmosphere referred to in the introduction to this section now returns to round it off.

The particular reference to the girl's **eyes** as **doves** has puzzled commentators a good deal – doves have been associated with so many things! It was a dove that brought good news to Noah with the olive leaf after the flood had receded (Gen. 8:11). Goulder notes that doves often consort in pairs which makes them a suitable image for this poem. He also notes that a dove's tail-feathers, when spread out, flutter like eyes. Fox cites one medieval commentator who called doves "the most enticing of all animals in matters of desire". In 4:1 the girl's eyes peep through the veil like doves – a reference to the shyness of doves, which hide away in clefts among rocks (see 2:14).

Gerleman considers the ogling looks of the lovers to resemble the light agility of doves – this is hardly likely, one feels, as ogling looks are surely slow and reluctant to move. However, in his commentary on a later passage (4:1) he makes other suggestions which seem more likely. In neither passage is the article of comparison (*k*ᵉ) used ("your eyes are (like) doves"); this absence suggests a sudden impression such as you may receive from looking afresh at a work of art. Egyptian art followed certain stylistic conventions: eyes were given a linear clarity which resembled the contours of a bird's body. Here we may have another example of Egyptian background influencing the Song of Songs. Indeed, the comparison of eyes to doves may well have been as frequent in Heb. love poetry as it was in Egyptian; but that is not evident to us, because no other love poems from the classical period of Heb. literature have survived.

16. The girl makes her reply in words very similar to those of the man, yet going that bit further, adding **truly lovely**, where **truly** translates *'ap̄*, a Heb. particle often placed before an epithet to heighten it, rather like "also" or "even" in English. The same emphatic particle introduces **Our couch is green**. The climactic use of this word is missed if we do not realize that the word for **Our couch** (*'arsenu*) denotes in Am. 6:4 particularly stylish and magnificent couches used for feasting; so the couch here in Ca. 1:16 is not in any old bed! Are the couple then really in a bedroom, or are they merely imagining that their rustic rendezvous is a royal palace? Goulder believes that this verse implies that the royal bed was daily strewn with fresh, newly cut foliage and rushes: if this is correct, then the greenery may have taken over the girl's imagination, and a real chamber has become another rustic fiction.

17. It seems more likely, however, that, just as the young man becomes a king in v. 4, so here the lovers' meeting-place has become a royal palace. The **beams** and **rafters** of the structure are, however, made not of the usual oak or sycamore but rather of the costly cedar and pine used in royal palaces. Whatever the real trees were, the poet represents them here as materials signifying royal luxury.

The Heb. word for **our rafters** (*rāḥîṭēnû*) is unusual: the Septuagint translates it as "coffered roofs" and the Vulgate as "carved ceilings". A philologically equivalent word in Syriac (*rehtā*) can mean "a (race)course" and the Assyrian *râtu* means a channel off which water runs. The **beams** and **rafters** of the house probably formed the coffered ceiling: the rich woods which are named thus enhance the luxury. As *RSV* margin suggests, the meaning is uncertain and must be derived from the context. The mention of **cedar** as a building material recalls the richness of Solomon's temple, which was constructed from imported woods. Some think the reference to **cedar** may indicate that the Song had a northern origin, as cedars never grow in southern Palestine: even the word for **cedars** (*b*ᵉ*rōṯîm* for the more usual *b*ᵉ*rōšîm*) may show northern linguistic influence, with the northern Aramaic *t* used for the southern Heb. *š*. The mention of the southern En-gedi in v. 14 may show that we have two smaller units (vv. 12–14 from the south and vv. 15–17 from the north) here combined in a single poem. But this may be splitting the text up too much, as both the fertile En-gedi and the cedars of Lebanon were well enough known to serve as literary, almost proverbial, images.

HEIGHTENING COMPLIMENTS
2:1–7

A second *Bechreibungslied* (or "song of admiration", see introduction to 1:9–17) now follows which, with certain differences, recapitulates many of the motifs in 1:9–17: the lovers exchange mutual praise (2:1–3, cf. 1:9–11 and 15–16a); they embrace each other (2:6, cf. 1:13–14) lying on a couch (2:6, cf. 1:12, 16b) inside a house (2:4a, cf. 1:17). The poem is again a dialogue but, whereas in 1:9–17 the lovers addressed each other directly in the second person, here each refers to the other in the third person. This change of person justifies us in recognizing this unit as a separate poem. However, a further difference is the use of a "fading-out" technique at the end in 2:7 – a technique used also in Egyptian love poetry. An appeal, or even an adjuration, addressed by the girl to her friends, the ubiquitous "daughters of Jerusalem" already encountered in 1:5 (see introductory remarks to 1:5–8), closes the poem. A similar device is used also in 3:5 and 8:4.

2:1. The girl starts the sequence of comparisons modestly. The phrase **rose of Sharon** in the English translations has almost become proverbial. It may surprise readers that the Heb. word used here (*ḥ*ª*ḇaṣṣeleṯ*) certainly did not mean what we call a **rose**, a flower which was native to the Caucasus and did not appear south of that region until the time of the Seleucids in the 3rd century BC. Elsewhere in the OT this Heb. word occurs only once – in Isa. 35:1, where it is used as a figure for abundant growth: "the desert shall rejoice and blossom like the crocus". In fact "crocus", as suggested in the *RSV* margin, is probably the correct translation here: the crocus grew wild freely in Palestine, particularly in the plain of the **Sharon**, a fertile region on the Mediterranean side of the central mountain ridge which stretched from the Egyptian border right up to the promontory of Carmel. Certainly the poet is not describing a rare flower of outstanding beauty here. The girl feels she is only one among many; she is just one crocus among the thousands which carpet the ground in the spring. The Good News Bible translates: "I am only a wild flower", getting the sense well by adding to the Heb. the English word "only".

The word **lily** is of a very general application: the cognate word in Arabic can mean any brilliantly coloured flower. Certainly the white lily is not intended; in any case, this does not grow wild in Israel. Here we need some plant which grows in great abundance to balance the crocus in the first half of the verse. In 5:13 lilies are used to describe lips, so clearly red is the colour intended in that passage: the same may be true here. In the phrase **lily of the valleys** the plural **valleys** is probably generic: so a valley-lily is meant, i.e. the type of lily that grows in the valleys. Like the crocus, this would have been a very common wild flower.

The fragile **rose** and **lily** contrast starkly with the more robust **cedar** and **pine** in 1:17 at the close of the preceding poem. Gerleman suggests that this obvious contrast may be the reason why these two poems are placed next to each other in the compilation. We know little about the reasons for such juxtaposition: sometimes catchwords may be detected, but contrast can conceivably be another explanation.

2. The man takes up the girl's word **lily** and draws it out in complimentary terms, turning her modest self-appraisal into the highest praise: she surpasses all other girls as **a lily** surpasses **brambles**. The latter were frequently found in Israel and were used in fables. In 2 Kg. 14:9 Jehoash, king of Israel, sends a fable as a message to Amaziah, king of Judah, contrasting "a cedar on Lebanon" (presumably himself in the north) with "a thistle" (presumably Amaziah in the south). In the poetry of Job 31:40 "thorns" (*ḥōaḥ* – the same word as in this passage) and "foul weeds" are cited as unprofitable plants in contrast to wheat and barley. The man's loved one is not merely a flower among so many flowers: she is **a lily among brambles**.

3. The girl now replies in similar vein. Whereas in the previous verse her lover likened her to **a lily** standing out amid wild vegetation, she now likens him not to a small flower but rather to an **apple tree** standing out **among the trees of the wood**. Some doubt exists about the reading, **apple tree**: cultivated apples are a comparatively recent development in Israel. But this is not a tree cultivated specially in a garden or orchard: it is wild **among the trees of the wood**. The Heb. word for **apple** (*tappūaḥ*) is used in the OT as among "trees of the field" (i.e. wild trees) in Jl. 1:12, for round golden ornaments set in silver (Prov. 25:11) and as the name of two cities (Jos. 12:17; 15:34; 16:8; 17:7). So there certainly existed a fruit known as the *tappūaḥ* (this is also the modern Heb. word for "apple"). It was found on certain trees in the wild and bore fruit with a rather acid, bitter-sweet taste and, it seems, aphrodisiac properties (as in 2:5; 7:9; 8:5). Apples were reputed to have special significance in Sumerian marriage mythology, and similar erotic qualities are attributed to apples elsewhere. Whether the *tappūaḥ* was related to the modern apple or to the apricot (as some think, cf. *NEB*) must remain uncertain. Even today some have sung "Don't go under the apple tree with anyone else but me" (Pope)!

With great delight I sat translates two Heb. verbs which are exactly parallel in construction and are joined by *w*^{e}, "and": *ḥimmaḏtî w*^{e}*yāšaḇtî.* Where such near-asyndetic constructions are used in Heb., the second verb (here **I sat**) indicates the main action, while the first (lit. "I delighted") implies some special aspect of the action, rather like an adverb (*G-K* § 120d). There is a similar case in Gen. 24:18, *watt*^{e}*maher wattôreḏ* (lit. "and she hurried and let (her jar) drop"), used of Rebekah giving a drink to Abraham's servant. The comparison between the lover and the tree yields two points of likeness: the girl sits in the shade of the tree, i.e. in the company of her lover, and tastes sweet fruit, i.e. enjoying the kisses of his mouth. In 1:13 he was a bag of myrrh lying between her breasts; now the situation is reversed, and he is a tree in whose sheltering shade she sits.

4. We take vv. 4–7 as a continuation of the dialogue of mutual admiration which began in vv. 1–3. It can be seen gradually to escalate until a wish for the very closest kind of physical contact is expressed in v. 6. In the whole section (vv. 1–6) **He brought me** is the only finite verb referring to an action expressed in the perfect tense and, apart from the two verbs in v. 3 (translated in *RSV* as **With great delight I sat**, and described above as "in near asyndeton"), there are no other verbs in vv. 1–3: all are descriptive nominal clauses without any signification of time. The two verbs in v. 3 refer clearly to a past situation of close friendship which led to the girl's present desires. Two major ancient versions disagree over the tense of **He brought me**: Vulg. translates the verb in the perfect tense (as *RSV*), but LXX has an imperative ("bring me into . . .") and caps it with a second imperative ("set love over me"), in line with the imperatives read by all witnesses in v. 5.

In v. 5 the girl is still waiting and longing for some physical demonstration of love in the future: has entry **to the banqueting house** already happened (so the perfect tense in MT and Vulg.) as a stage towards the climax, or is this entry part of the future she longs for so passionately (so LXX)? This choice is made more difficult by the fact that these two forms (the perfect *h*^{e}*ḇî'ănī*, **He brought me**, and the imperative *h*^{a}*ḇî'ēnī*, "Bring me!") were written identically in the consonantal Heb. text which existed before the vowel points were added; thus the text was open to either interpretation. If we vocalize the verb as a perfect with *RSV*, the girl has already been brought **to the banqueting house** as a further stage towards the climax of her love; if we vocalize it as an imperative, such an entry is still only part of her dream for the future. Exactly which stage she has reached either in her dreams or in reality, we cannot decide definitely: each interpretation has its own merits.

the banqueting house is a rather ornate translation of the Heb. *bēṯ hayyayin*, "a house" or "a place of wine"; for *bēṯ* can mean, as well as a house, simply a place in general, or even an animal's lair. The Heb. may then indicate any place where wine is drunk – perhaps even the rustic arbour which is the lovers' rendezvous (after all, in the earlier imagery this became a royal palace). Certainly, as Fox points out, a banqueting hall seems out of place in poems where the theme is so often separation from the city (see *VT* 33 (1983), pp. 201–2). A city context is envisaged in 3:1–4, but in a quite explicit way.

But Rudolph and Gerleman have other ideas: Arabic drinking and love poetry sometimes speaks of a sign being put up outside a house, giving notice that a drinking party is to be held and that guests are welcome. Curious links like this often exist between customs in pre-Islamic Arab society and early Hebrew practices, so that this parallel may prove worth following up – the whole point of the imagery being that the **banner** over this particular rendezvous is not for drinking, but for **love**! This interpretation seems to fit the rural context well.

Interpretations have varied a good deal, however. Elsewhere *diḡlô*, the Heb. word for his **banner**, is used only in the Pentateuch of tribal military standards. LXX translated *diḡlô* as a verb ("set up (love) over me"), taking seriously the more common meaning of the noun *deḡel* as a military standard and reading the piel imperative of the cognate verb (*dagg*ᵉ*lû*). Fox and Gordis compare the Accadian verb *dagalu*, "to look upon, behold", and the noun *diglu*, "glance, look, intent". Fox then takes **love** as suggesting love-making and translates (like Pope): "his intent towards me was love". This is similar to *NEB*: "and (he) gave me loving glances".

5. Sustain me with raisins strikes the reader as odd. Perhaps the raisins are a health food to help the girl recover from love-sickness, as she confesses she is **sick with love**? But what she needs is not to maintain her strength at its normal level but rather to be braced and strengthened for the coming experience. Thus *NEB* with its talk of refreshing with raisins seems too weak. The Heb. verb (*samm*ᵉ*ḵûnî*) is in the piel, a verbal form often used of frequentative or strengthening action: Gordis ("strengthen me") has the right nuance, as do Gerleman and Rudolph (both *stärket mich*). Fox translates quite differently, however: "put me to bed (among the fruit clusters)". He claims that the piel of this verb (used only here in the Bible) is used "occasionally in Mishnaic Hebrew" of preparing a bed; but he gives no examples, referring readers to Jastrow's dictionary of rabbinic Hebrew. Certainly the cognate noun, *s*ᵉ*mîḵāh*, is used in Jg. 4:18 of something which Jael threw over Sisera to conceal him from his enemies, and Jewish exegetical tradition thought this was a rug or a goat-hair curtain (Burney suggested that it was a fly-net, but that would hardly conceal anyone!). This seems to be the only connexion of this root with beds or blankets, as Jastrow's dictionary gives no such meaning as Fox claims. So we must reject Fox's suggestion, and see the girl as requesting some strengthening food.

For this purpose **raisins**, or more properly "raisin cakes" (*JB*), may seem somewhat inadequate. Raisin cakes, studded with raisins like the inflorescence of a palm tree (see G. R. Driver, *Festschrift für Alfred Bertholet*, p. 144), were a stimulating food given to the people in 2 Sam. 6:19 and 1 Chr. 16:3. Such cakes are sarcastically condemned by Hosea (3:1); it seems they were used in the Baal cult as aphrodisiacs. They were used in pagan worship by the Moabites also (Isa. 16:7). So the girl in her weakness asks for real food, but the aphrodisiac nature of the food she specifically asks for shows that she wants it both ways! She requests food which will strengthen her physically, but which will also increase her desire and thus her weakness. She also asks for apples, another food with alleged aphrodisiac properties (see on v. 3).

6. In this verse there is no verb: two nominal clauses describe the circumstances attendant on the girl being "sick with love"

(v. 5). *RSV* starts the verse with a wish formula: **O that his left hand were under my head**: but there is no indication in the Heb. of a wish or of the construction usual for wishes (*mî yitten*, lit. "Who will give . . . ?", idiomatically meaning "Oh that . . . !"). No other modern translation takes it as *RSV*, nor do LXX or Vulg. The verse should be taken as a factual description of the positions of the two lovers; cf. *NIV*: "his left arm is under my head, and his right arm embraces me". Lying passively in her lover's shadow (v. 3), the girl has been brought into just the right setting for love (v. 4); she then asks for apples and raisins – both erotic fruits in Heb. tradition. This verse then forms the climax before the closing adjuration to the daughters of Jerusalem. Surely, instead of inventing a wish, we should take the Heb. as it is – describing how she now lies in a position suitable for making love: her lover's **left hand** is **under** her **head** and his **right hand** embraces her. Whether in a dream or in reality, she now lies in her lover's embrace, ready for love. As Rudolph notes, this verse confirms that the **banner** in v. 4 should be interpreted as an inn sign: she has now reached the threshold of the secrets of love.

In the English translations the situation envisaged in this verse (i.e. the lovers being on the verge of making love) is identical to that in 8:3. Also, 2:7 and 8:4 are almost the same. In the original Heb. text the expression **under** is spelt in 8:3 *taḥaṯ* and here *l^e^ṯaḥaṯ*, prefixed by the lesser preposition *l^e^*; but this makes no difference to the meaning.

7. In this verse the **daughters of Jerusalem** reappear. They first appeared in 1:5, where they seemed to be just a convenient third party other than the lover whom the girl could address. They exist only for the girl's convenience – she has to air her thoughts and feelings to someone! So the poet conveniently provides an almost Greek-type chorus – it is a literary topos, an artistic means to express the girl's thoughts. The **daughters of Jerusalem** are thus just stage figures. Similar stylistic devices are found in Egyptian poetry: family relatives, rivals in love and even dangerous beasts or separating waters are appealed to in this way in differing contexts.

The wording of this verse occurs two other times in the Song, in 3:5 and 8:4. It is useful to note the contexts of those two verses. 8:3 is almost identical to 2:6, as noted above, and in 8:1–2 the girl dreams of leading her lover into an inner chamber (**the chamber of her that conceived me**) and giving him intoxicating drinks (figurative for the intoxication of loving embraces?) – all very similar to 3:4, where she finds him after roaming the streets in the middle of the night and drags him off to the same **chamber of her that conceived** her. Both passages break off before any mention of sexual acts and interject this refrain from the daughters of Jerusalem. In 1:5 the girl only comments to them coyly on her personal appearance, but in the other three passages she adjures them to **stir not up nor awaken love until it please**. In all three passages the context is that of sexual love which is about to take place. Some scholars have suggested that aphrodisiac drugs are involved, but the contexts in all three passages show that the girl is well aroused and has no need of such stimulants. Her wish, then, is not to stop others stirring up love until it please, but rather to stop them disturbing love-making; cf. Gordis: "that you will not disturb nor interrupt our love until it be satiated", taking *tĕḥpāṣ* as "(until) it wishes (to be disturbed)".

She adjures them **by the gazelles or the hinds of the field**. **the field** (*hassāḏeh*) means simply the open country, so she adjures them by the wild animals. The Heb. verb is the hiphil of *šaḇaʿ*, usually used of making people swear or putting them on oath. How seriously are we to take this? It seems strange to find a biblical writer making people swear **by the gazelles or the hinds of the field**: Fox mentions Mesopotamian magic spells which cite gazelles as the very epitome of sexual potency, and Loretz claims that such imagery was common in the love lyrics of the ancient Orient. A further play on words may be detected here, for the Heb. words for **gazelles** and **hinds of the field** are very similar to certain expressions for God. In fact, "(Lord of) hosts" and **gazelles** have the same consonants and vowels (*ṣᵉḇāʾōṯ*), and **the hinds of the field** (*ʾaylōṯ hassāḏeh*) closely resembles *ʾēl šadday*, "God Almighty". It may be true, as Ringgren suggests, that hinds and gazelles were traditional terms in a fixed formula concerning pagan cultic marriages, and that such mythical traits may lie behind the Song. But Fox suggests that here animal names which resemble divine titles may be used to avoid explicit reference to God in a secular context. If Fox is right in this, then this is the first sign of a tendency, particularly prominent in the later Talmudic period, to make substitutions for divine names and titles in oaths, thus avoiding use of apparent divine titles in a secular context. **hinds** and **gazelles** are also mentioned here because the sound of their names resembles divine titles; but they also excellently suit the rustic character of the poems.

THE LOVER SHUT OUT
2:8–17

Most of this unit consists of the words which the young man sings outside his beloved's window while he stands hopefully waiting for her to come out and enjoy the pleasures of spring with him. The words are all set in the mouth of the beloved, who describes her lover's enthusiastic arrival (vv. 8f.) and then retells the song he sings outside her door: this starts in v. 10 and extends into v. 14. The beloved's response to her lover is clearly contained in vv. 16f., but it remains uncertain whether v. 15 is part of the lover's song to his beloved (as indicated by the quotation marks in *RSV*) or a (rather strange?) response from the beloved before her speech in vv. 16f. That vv. 8–17 should be treated as a single unit is shown by the repetition of v. 9's **gazelle** and **stag** in v. 17; this literary device, which is known as inclusion, seals the unit off rather like brackets.

The lover's song closely resembles the classical *paraklausithyron*, a special kind of song found in Greek and especially Latin lyric poetry. Good examples are found in Aristophanes, Callimachus, Lucretius, Catullus, Horace, Tibullus and especially Propertius. Such songs were particularly popular in Rome. That this form of lyric poetry was well known is shown by the presence of a Greek comic playwright in this list. These classical poems are discussed by E. Burck, "Das Paraklausithyron: die Entwicklungsgeschichte eines Motivs der antiken Liebesdichtung" in *Das Humanistische Gymnasium* 43 (1932), pp. 186–200 and by F. O. Copley, *Exclusus Amator* (1956). Copley states that "the earliest extant example of the dramatic *paraklausithyron* is from Aristophanes' *Ecclesiazusae* (lines 938–75)" (p. 7), never mentioning this example in the Song of Songs. More significantly, he does not mention the Egyptian examples, some of which Fox quotes, especially nos. 46 and 47 (pp. 75–7). It is thus plain that the *paraklausithyron* existed in Egyptian love lyrics well before Aristophanes, as the papyrus cited by Fox dates from the 20th dynasty (c. 12th century BC). Whether there is any direct influence from the Egyptian songs on the Greek authors is difficult to say, but Copley's account is certainly incomplete in this respect. Clearly, we have here another example of the Song reflecting Egyptian literary fashions.

8. The voice of my beloved! *RSV* here probably misinterprets the Heb. *qōl*, "voice". Though the word may be used elliptically for "I hear a sound" (cf. Goulder's "I hear his call"), it is more probably an exclamation (cf. Gen. 4:10) – virtually an imperative like "Hark! my beloved!" (*NEB*, cf. *AB*) or "Listen! my beloved . . ." (Fox). To translate this word as an exclamation is preferable to *RSV*, as there is no record of his **voice** actually being heard until he has arrived (v. 10) after all his dashing about.

In **Behold, he comes** the demonstrative pronoun *zeh*, usually "this", is used as an enclitic (cf. *G-K* § 136d). It could perhaps be rendered most easily by the English enclitic "now": "See, now, he comes!" Some have suggested that the words **leaping** and **bounding** refer to nature deities, but such an interpretation is unnecessary: this is poetry, and such words illustrate very well the young man's eagerness to reach his beloved. Both Heb. verbs are very graphic: *m*ᵉ*ḏallēg*, **leaping**, is used of a stag in Isa. 35:6; *m*ᵉ*qappēṣ*, **bounding**, means literally "drawing together", describing the repeated contractions of muscles in making leaps; cf. the cognate Arabic *qafaza*, used of antelopes, gazelles and horses. These scenic expressions maintain the rustic imagery of the Song, and it seems idle to restrict the setting of the lover's keenness to "running across the undulating palace garden", as Goulder does: the poetic imagery envisages real mountains. The reference to **leaping** and **bounding** nicely prepares the way for the actual mention of the **gazelle** and **stag** in the next verse.

9. The comparison suggested by the verbs used in the previous verse is now made more explicit: **My beloved is like a gazelle, or a young stag**. The animals cited suggest the lover's speed in coming; cf. 2 Sam. 2:18, where "Asahel was as swift of foot as a wild gazelle". But that comparison lies perhaps not only in speed, but also in the power of the gazelle's sexual desire: Felix claims that in the spring buck frequently wander round the hill-country seeking mates. Fox cites an Egyptian love song (no. 40, pp. 66f.) in which the girl compares her lover's haste in coming to her to the speed of a running gazelle. But the connotation is different: in the Song the emphasis is on the lover's grace and handsomeness; in the Egyptian song, pursued by a hunter, he seeks a quiet haven. The different animals described in this verse are studied by G. R. Driver in *Festschrift für Alfred Bertholet*, p. 134, to which article animal lovers are directed. The **gazelle** and **young stag** serve as catchwords that link this poem to the previous one, where **gazelles** and **hinds** (same Heb. word as for **young stag** here) are mentioned (v. 7).

The lover **stands behind our wall**, and the girl is waiting inside the house. The Heb. word for **lattice** occurs only here in the OT. G. R. Driver thought it referred to an ancient Semitic custom still surviving in what the Arabs today call *mašrabiyya*, balconies shaded with lattice-work which lets in air but not light and through which you can just peep. Certainly LXX's "(fishing or hunting) nets" and Aquila's "network" imply some such arrangement.

10. My beloved speaks: After a series of descriptive participles comes *'ānāh* in the perfect tense – literally, "he answered". This clearly lies in sequence between his arrival (vv. 8–9) and his speech (vv. 10–15). Some scholars suggest revocalizing *'ānāh* to read the participle *'ōneh* to match the rest of the sequence, but it is more likely that the poet used a perfect tense deliberately to break the sequence of participles and indicate something new happening.

When the lover begins his *paraklausithyron*, his words do not directly fit the classical pattern in Greek and Latin literature. He waits outside, not admitted to the delights of love within, trying to persuade his beloved to come out to him. His song contains nothing specific on the delights of their love relationship and he brings no garland of flowers to throw on her doorstep, as he would do in a Roman poem: rather he celebrates the freshness of the Palestinian spring. Ringgren rightly thought it a waste of time to hunt for erotic undertones in poems like this. References to animals and flowers appear everywhere in the Song: Falk has detected over twenty-five varieties of trees, shrubs, flowers, nuts and spices (cf. pp. 97–106). Such a profusion of references to nature, she claims, suggests a "readiness to respond to sensuality": love awakes as the world of nature awakes. Springtime has always had romantic connotations. As an English madrigal puts it, "Sweet lovers love the spring."

11. the winter in Palestine is the rainy season, so the two halves of this verse are neatly balanced and parallel. But note that this reference to nature has nothing to do with celebrating God's creation explicitly or with Canaanite fertility religion (as the prophets sometimes suggest), and there are no mythical overtones: spring is celebrated in a purely lyrical way. **rain** in Palestine is confined almost completely to the winter months of Europe, and the time referred to here, as Fox notes, is May or June, when vines and figs begin to ripen and when migrant birds appear. Several linguistic points add to the striking nature of the poetic style: the word for **winter**, *s*^{e}*ṯāyw*, occurs in the Bible only here and is an Aramaism. The phrase, **is over and gone** translates two verbs, *ḥālăp̱ hālăḵ*, used in asyndeton to heighten the effect. As Pope says, "the rainy season is completely past, over and gone". Gordis suggested that the link with spring, the time of the Passover festival, may have been the reason for the reading of the Song at that festival; but it seems strange that such an unhistorical collection of poems should be read at a festival which concentrated so much on historical deliverance. However, this practice may account for the allegorizing policy followed in the Targum, where everything in the Song is interpreted in terms of Israel's history.

12. This verse describes three signs of spring. First, it pictures the sudden blooming of flowers in the Palestinian countryside: **The flowers appear on the earth** almost like a carpet in some areas. This sudden flowering forms a complete contrast both to the cold, wet winter and to the arid late summer. The third sign of spring is also easy to understand: **the turtledove** is a migratory bird which is said in Jer. 8:7 to "keep the time of" its "coming" like the stork, the swallow and the crane. Lys claims that its cooing can be heard in Palestine from March/April – maybe the return of this bird could easily be recognized as a sign of the seasons like the first cuckoo in spring?

The second sign of spring is less easy to interpret, as the phrase *'ēṯ hazzāmîr* can be (and has been) translated with equal correctness as both "the time of pruning" (cf. LXX, Pesh., Vulg., Gerleman) and **the time of singing** (cf. *NEB*, *JB*, *GNB*, Gordis, Fox and medieval commentators). The Heb. word can bear each meaning equally well, and so we must interpret according to the context: the context of v. 11 is that of the time of year, and clearly favours "pruning"; the second half of v. 12 refers to the cooing **voice of the turtledove**, which suggests **singing** for *hazzāmîr*. The phrase suits both contexts well (there is no need to introduce the idea of circumcision into the interpretation, as the Midrash does!) and points both ways. This matter was taken up by Cyrus H. Gordon ("New Directions", *Bulletin of the American Society of Papyrologists* 15 (1978), pp. 59f.), who suggested that *zāmîr* contained a deliberate double reference, backwards to the change of seasons in the agricultural year and forwards to the birds' song in summer. This kind of effect he called "Janus parallelism" after the Roman god Janus, who had two faces looking opposite ways.

There were two times for pruning in Palestine: March and June. The March pruning would be too early to suit the "vines in blossom" in the next verse. The Gezer calendar, an ancient (10th century BC) inscription giving a list of months for different agricultural activities, places the "months of pruning" in between the wheat harvest and the harvest of summer fruit. So Gordon may be right: this double Janus-like meaning of *zāmîr* would provide a neat link between the departure of the rain and the appearance of the wild flowers (both in v. 11), and the singing of newly migrated birds (end of v. 12).

13. The first half of this verse bristles with difficulties. The reference to figs and vine blossoms concerns times suitable for making love, as the references to the natural world in vv. 11–13 are bracketed by the exhortation, **Arise, my love, my fair one,**

and come away, a phrase which acts as a refrain in this poem.

The problems start with the Heb. verb *ḥānᵉṭāh*, here translated **puts forth**. Elsewhere in the OT this verb is used only twice, in both cases of embalming: of Jacob in Gen. 50:2 and of Joseph in Gen. 50:26. The cognate verb in Arabic, *ḥanaṭa*, "became mature", in the intensive form means "embalmed", and nouns derived from it mean "spices" for a corpse and "embalmer". Syriac, Aramaic and Ethiopic words from this root also mean "embalm". It is the ancient versions (LXX, Vulg., Pesh.) which translate "put forth": either they didn't recognize the meaning or they couldn't see the relevance of embalming here. Embalming is effected by the infusion of aromatic mixtures into the corpse: perhaps we may suggest, with Fox, that what this verb suggests is the fig-tree sending fragrant sap through its limbs into the hard, unripe figs. The Heb., *păggîm*, is thought to denote the small, hard, green figs which are carried over from the winter and which then change colour in May/June. In contemporary Palestine the cognate Arabic *fegg* is used of the primary stage in the development of the early fig, and Mishnaic Heb. uses the word *păggāh* for a hard, unripe fig.

So it is not the "putting forth" of the unripe fig that suits the sense here – that is not a sign of spring. Rather, the author remarks on the change of colour that marks the fig's ripening. The time of the fig's appearance is by no means as significant as the time of its ripening in early summer. Thus translations which interpret this phrase as referring to ripening are to be preferred: "The fig ripens her fruits" (*AB*); "figs are beginning to ripen" (*GNB*); "the figs' ripening is at hand" (Goulder); Gerleman's translation is even better, since it specifically mentions the change of colour: "has coloured (*gefärbt*) its fruits." According to the Greek biologist Theophrastus, in antiquity much interest was shown in the different colourings of the fig; some even regarded the change of colour at ripening as miraculous.

The problems in this verse continue with the word *sᵉmāḏăr*, here translated **in blossom**: it has no preposition and seems to be used as a predicate in a verbless noun clause (*G-K* § 141d). It is used in a similarly predicative way in 2:15 of vines, and in 7:13 apparently of blossom opening (its buds?). G. R. Driver thought the word meant the small cup of deciduous leaves on the vine plant which later opened up into blossom; but he noted also that the halves of the poetic line here are not equally balanced: if *s^{e}māḏăr* were omitted, **The fig tree puts forth its figs, and the vines . . . give forth fragrance** would balance perfectly. So he concluded that *s^{e}māḏăr* had been inserted here as an explanatory gloss from other occurrences of the word, i.e. the vines give fragrance when they are in blossom. It is interesting that a wine jar discovered at Hazor had *SMDR* inscribed on it – so perhaps *s^{e}māḏăr* was the name of a type of wine (cf. Y. Yadin, *BA* 20 (1957), p. 40).

14. In 1:15 the lover compared his beloved's eyes to doves: now he addresses her in the vocative as **my dove**, as in 5:2 and 6:9. "My dove" is used as a term of endearment in classical Greek and Latin writings, and the dove has been a universal symbol of peace for a very long time. But it is also the love-bird *par excellence* and was in Greek lore the symbol of Ishtar, Atargatis and Aphrodite, the goddesses of love. Archaeologists found images of doves in the remains of a shrine to Astarte at Beth Shean. Doves and parts of doves were used in love magic even in the Middle Ages. For more material on doves see G. R. Driver in *PEQ* 1955, pp. 129f.

the clefts of the rock and **the covert of the cliff** appear to have been favourite places for doves to hide. In Jer. 49:16 the people of Edom are said to live "in the clefts of the rock", trying vainly to find a hiding-place where they will be beyond Yahweh's reach. Inaccessibility is also implied in Ob. 3, where the same phrase occurs. In all three passages the Heb. wording is the same: *ḥăgwē (has)sela'*.

The Heb. word for **covert** is *maḏrēgāh*, etymologically related to the Arabic word *darajatu(n)*, "stair"; the Aramaic and Syriac *dargā* also means "stair" or "step". In the Arabic and Assyrian words derived from this root the sense is one of height rather than simply of inaccessibility, and in later Heb. the word even came to mean "rank". The implication behind the word **covert** appears to be step-like terracing constructed to assist agriculture in rocky mountain areas – a technique to be seen widely in modern Israel. Probably *NEB* is more accurate here with "(my dove . . . that hides . . .) in crannies on the high ledges".

The lover asks to **see** his beloved's **face** and to **hear** her **voice** – very proper, polite requests which would most naturally come at the end of a polite speech. They are answered by the girl's very teasing retort in v. 15. That verse is difficult to interpret on any reading, but it probably makes better sense if we regard it not as the conclusion of the lover's speech (so *RSV*) but as a coquettish response from the girl (so Fox with a query).

15. If this verse is regarded as following vv. 10–14 in the same poem (so *RSV*), then it makes better sense from the mouth of the beloved than it does from the mouth of the lover (as *RSV*), particularly if she has run off to rocky **clefts** which even **little foxes** would reach only with difficulty. Foxes were notorious in the ancient world for damaging vineyards. Notable is a passage in Theocritus' *Idylls* 1.49; there Gow's commentary gives a list of classical references to damage caused by foxes – references ranging from Aesop to Varro and including this passage from the Song. At the end of Gow's commentary is a plate which reproduces a scaraboid of a fox spoiling a vine. The destructive behaviour of foxes was well known to Hebrew readers too: in Neh. 4:3 Tobiah the Ammonite speaks sarcastically of foxes breaking down the new wall around Jerusalem; and Ezekiel, condemning false prophets, says they "have been like foxes among ruins" (13:4) – a remark which, in Zimmerli's view, suggests that the destructiveness of foxes was proverbial. Certainly such a common proverbial usage would explain the wide spread of similar references in the ancient world. Some ancient sources also suggest that foxes are particularly fond of grapes. As vineyards have already appeared in the Song as symbols of the maiden's chastity (cf. 1:6, where she has **not kept** her vineyard), these **little foxes** are probably unscrupulous male admirers of the girl, whom her lover must keep in check in order to protect her. The poet indulges in not a little erotic playfulness at this point.

The foxes are given extra emphasis by the poet's use of repetitive parallelism of the single-word type – that is, he repeats **the foxes**. Cf. similar repetitions in the Song of Deborah in Jg. 5 ("fought" four times in vv. 19–20, "galloping" twice in v. 22, "he sank, he fell" twice in v. 27). This is a feature of ancient poetic style which is found also in the northern Ps. 29 in vv. 1–

2, 3–5 and 7–9 and in Ugaritic, cf. W. F. Albright, "Archaic Survivals in the Text of Canticles", *Hebrew and Semitic Studies presented to G. R. Driver* (Oxford, 1963), pp. 2f.

16. Close upon the ravaging foxes comes a phrase from the girl which through a "formula of mutual longing" (A. Feuillet) expresses the complete reciprocity of the relationship between her and the lover. It is hardly right to read into the use of this formula the religious covenant formula as used, for example, in Jer. 7:23, 11:4, Ezek. 34:30, etc.; it is surely more likely that this phrase describes the symbolic unity of the sexual relationship, and that the prophets used this conjugal symbolism to describe the closeness of the covenant. Ringgren points to parallel uses of similar phrases in the ancient Gilgamesh epic and in modern Arabic love poetry – both non-theological contexts. The poet uses the phrase here specifically to describe the contented unity the lovers feel after the attempted spoiling by the **foxes**.

Pasturing **his flock among the lilies** may seem a strange thing for the lover to do! As Feuillet remarks, "it is not usually in a bed of lilies that one leads a flock to feed" (*RB* 68 (1961), p. 9). Others have seen the bed of lilies as metaphorically signifying the girl's lips or breasts. But this treats the poetry as a too literal allegory; surely a poet may use a particular background without being accused of using allegory. Within the whole background of these poems the poet uses playful, unreal fiction in this way to express a lover's enjoyment of his beloved. The imagery remains imagery: this is poetry, not prose.

17. The time of day intended by the words, **Until the day breathes and the shadows flee** is uncertain. In some climates the day "breathing" would naturally refer to the fresh breeze of morning before the heat of the day comes on. The *GNB* writes this time of day into its translation: "until the morning breezes blow and the darkness disappears". But does the author by mentioning this flight of shadows intend us to think of them getting ever shorter until the sun stands theoretically directly overhead at noon, casting no shadow at all on the ground? Surely this phenomenon is not well described by the words, **the shadows flee**. It is probably better to envisage shadows lengthening later in the day, when the sun sinks towards the horizon: they then seem to rush away from you ever more speedily along the ground until the sun has finally set. Scholars have taken it both ways. Rudolph claimed that the lengthening shadows of evening seem to flee away; Fox, however, questions the logic of this. For him shadows don't flee in the evening – they rather stretch out longer and longer and disappear in the morning at midday when the sun is directly overhead. Goulder also assumes that the breeze referred to is the morning breeze, and that the girl is inviting her lover to spend the night with her.

But climatic conditions vary with geographical location. There seems to me no doubt that **the shadows flee** in the evening, but how does this fit in with the day breathing? I was once at Tiberias during the late afternoon of a very hot day, and there I enjoyed the strong, refreshing breeze from the west which cleared away the stifling heat of the day. One felt that one could breathe again, and so it could be said that the day breathed afresh after its earlier stifling closeness. Certainly the problem of interpretation grows the more you think about it: why should the lovers separate before evening comes, with its welcome darkness? Perhaps they were enjoying privacy at siesta-time, when no one was around! Fox is probably right to detect some *double entendre* here, though for me the refreshing breeze at Tiberias tips the scale for the late afternoon. We should note a fine interpretative translation in Pesh.: "until the day grows cool (*n*ᵉ*p̄ûḡ*)". The translator of Pesh. knew his climatic and geographical conditions well!

A further problem is presented by the **rugged mountains** (*hārēy bāṯĕr*) traversed by the **young stag**. The Heb. root here translated **rugged** (*bāṯĕr*, or rather *bĕṯĕr* with the first vowel lengthened in the pause at the end of the verse) is used in Gen. 15:10 and Jer. 34:18–19 only of halves of animals cut in two in the making of covenants: the idea of division is therefore thought to belong closely to the root, whence the **rugged mountains** are seen as divided from each other by deep valleys or gorges. Not even the ancient translators knew what was going on here! LXX has "valleys" (clefts between hills), Theodotian has "spices", Aquila and Vulg. both transliterate, and the Hexapla has a corrupted Greek form clearly originating from *malabathron*, the name of an aromatic spice from India which Pliny, the Roman student of natural history, said was found in Egypt and Syria. Worthy of note is the fact that the first half of 4:6 is exactly the same as the first half of this verse, but the latter part of 4:6 reads, **I will hie me to the mountain of myrrh and the hill of frankincense**. Pliny's spice, *malabathron*, probably provides the key to understanding *bĕṯĕr* here as a fragrant spice.

But what of the **mountains**? Are we to think of them as "the cloven hills" of the girl's "breast" (Goulder)? They can hardly be her *mons veneris* (Haupt), as there must be more than one: such sexual ingenuity does not help. Elsewhere the hills are associated with spices, as in 4:6 (twice) and 8:14; in these lyric poems the association of mountains with sweet-smelling spices seems to have been a reasonably common topos. Gerleman reminds us that Egyptian love poetry frequently refers to a distant land named Punt (probably in South Arabia) which was famed for all kinds of spices. So famous was Punt for such luxurious products that its name became a literary topos in itself. Fox includes one particularly good example among the Egyptian love songs which he quotes:

All birds of (the land of) Punt –
they have descended into Egypt,
anointed with myrrh.
The first to come
takes my bait.
His fragrance is brought from Punt:
his claws are full of balm.

(no. 9 on pp. 16f.)

Compare also another (less textually certain) example, no. 20F on p. 33. So, Gerleman claims, the **rugged mountains** of Beṯer may in this song be a half-legendary wonderland like Punt in Egyptian poetry; they are mentioned here in order to arouse sensual feeling – the **gazelle** is referred to for the same reason. This suggestion may be right – we have little other Heb. lyric poetry to compare for such usages. If Beṯer is indeed the name of a place famed for luxury products like spices, we should acknowledge that Vulg. may have recognized this correctly with its transliteration *Bether*.

A HAPPY DREAM
3:1–5

This section narrates nocturnal experiences of the girl, and closes with a renewed appeal to the daughters of Jerusalem. The sequence of events is clear. The girl feels compassionate longing for her beloved in the middle of the night: she calls for him but receives no reply, so she gets up and searches for him in the streets of the town. As she does so she encounters the town guard doing their night rounds. Soon after that she finds her beloved and takes him off to her mother's house (not an unlikely place for such a rendezvous in Egyptian and Sumerian poetry). This section closes, as do several others, with an appeal to the daughters of Jerusalem not to disturb the couple's love-making.

As Gerleman notes, this account is all rather unlikely and bizarre – it is risky for a girl to wander through the streets in the middle of the night even these days, with street-lighting – it was even riskier then! However, these verses are not as bizarre as the appearance of the night guard in 5:7, where they apparently take the girl's clothes off and beat her! Ringgren finds this lonely nocturnal search quite unrealistic – not at all suitable, he suggests, for relating or performing at a wedding. But for him such problems disappear if we recognize an original cultic song underlying this particular poem. In this song a goddess seeks a male god who has disappeared (or died); she finds him and then brings him back to the bridal chamber in her mother's house. Ringgren finds similar cultic songs in the Babylonian Tammuz/Ishtar myth and the Egyptian Isis/Osiris myth, both of which were known in Canaan. But Tammuz died and came back to life – no death or return to life is mentioned here. And the ritual search for Tammuz was carried out with weeping – there is no hint of ritual weeping here. In the absence of such prominent elements, that interpretation seems most unlikely.

O. Loretz rightly remarks that in the ancient Orient it was unthinkable for a girl to wander about alone like this. That was probably the case in reality, but this is a dream, and dreams are thought to reveal our subconscious longings, particularly when we are in love. Thoughts and desires which we try to banish from our minds often surface at night, and this is probably so in this dream. So it is no surprise to find certain recurrent ideas dominating the dream narrated in this poem: "him whom my soul loves" (vv. 1, 2, 3 and 4), and seeking but not finding (vv. 1, 2) culminating in finding (v. 4). This seeking but not finding is emphasized by an ironic twist: though she is seeking her lover, the town guard find *her*. However, although the girl's wandering in the streets seems suitable as part of a dream, Egyptian love poetry certainly recognized a tendency for lovers to behave strangely, as shown by Fox's poem no. 34 (pp. 53f.).

3:1. Lying upon her bed, the girl longed desperately for her lover. She may still have been dreaming: she may not have literally **sought him** with her hand and found him gone (as Goulder, but cf. J. T. Willis, *Biblica* 48 (1967), pp. 537f.). The two prepositional phrases at the head of the sentence describe the subject of the clause, the girl, rather than the seeking. Rudolph brings this out well by inserting a participle in his translation: "By night (lying) upon my bed, I sought . . ." A dream of searching hardly *begins* when, awake without her lover, she tries to suppress thoughts of loneliness: such dreams (perhaps products of wishful thinking) happen rather when she is already asleep. Because of the plural form of the Heb. word translated **by night** (*ballēylōṯ*), some have thought that the verse is speaking about anxieties which are recurrent "night after night" (so *NEB*, *GNB*, Fox). But the plural form here is a so-called plural of composition denoting not a succession of nights but rather night-time in general. To remark that the same dream often repeats itself anyway (so Rudolph) seems unnecessarily trite as an explanation.

The words, **I called him, but he gave no answer** occur in LXX but not in the Heb. *NEB* includes them, as does *RSV*, but most other translations omit them as a harmonizing gloss inserted from 5:6, where they follow exactly the same phrase as here. It is probable that they were added to make this verse conform to 5:6, particularly as both verses are closely related to dream sequences; it is less likely that the words in question were left out of the Heb. text by mistake. Gordis calls this kind of amendment "levelling". The two dream passages are certainly similar, but hardly identical; there is no justification for such tampering with the text. A better argument for reading these words here arises from the balance required in Heb. poetic form: frequently a statement in the first half of a poetic line is balanced by another statement in the second half. Here **I sought him . . .** is balanced by **I called him . . .**, as the arrangement of the two halves of the line in *RSV* indicates. Without **I called him . . .** the line would remain lopsided.

2. The girl receives no reply, so in her dream she starts her nocturnal expedition, searching for her beloved in the streets of the town. Notice the changed setting of this song: the first two chapters were rustic and pastoral, but now we have **streets** and **squares**. Goulder, treating the entire book as one continuous whole, thought the earlier rustic arbour represented the royal audience chamber; he said of the present passage "the palace and its corridors and spacious rooms are spoken of as a town with lanes and streets" (p. 27). But if we view the book as a collection of songs loosely linked on the Egyptian pattern, we need only recognize that the earlier songs presupposed a rustic setting, whereas here we find songs arising from a town situation. The location is hardly a **city**, as *RSV*, and it is certainly not Jerusalem; but it is large enough to have **streets** and **squares** for the girl to wander through in her search. As Pope implies, it is unnecessary nonsense to detect here a mythical designation of the netherworld.

There has been some discussion over the word **streets** (*šᵉwāqîm*): the Heb. is clearly linked to the Accadian *sūqū*, "street", and to well-known Arabic cognates such as *sûq*, "market place" (cf. M. Ellenbogen, *Foreign Words in the Old Testament* (1962), p. 158). The unusual broken plural form led H. Schmökel to revocalize *šôqîm*, "knees", and to detect a reference to going around on one's knees expressing prolonged seeking – a form of knee ambulation depicted on cylinder seals. This Pope rightly rejects as "dubious in the extreme". Anyway, other nouns have similarly broken plurals, cf. *šᵉwārîm* in Hos. 12:12 and *dᵉwāḏîm* in 2 Chr. 35:13. Further, the plural of this word occurs only here, so there is no regular plural form in Heb. for comparison.

I sought him, but found him not: these words, repeated from the previous verse, appear in all the ancient versions and seem genuine. A. R. Ceresco (*CBQ* 44 (1982), pp. 551–69, especially pp. 552–5 and 564–8) cites these words as an example of *antanaclasis*, a form of paronomasia where the same word is repeated with a different meaning. The word *māṣā'*, he claims, is particularly suited to this rhetorical figure; it can mean both "found" and "reached, attained", these meanings corresponding to two quite different roots in Ugaritic: *mṣ'* and *mẓ'*. But C. H. Gordon in his *Ugaritic Textbook* (no. 1524 on p. 436) treats these forms as variants. Certainly the two senses hardly appear sufficiently different to justify any such bold rhetorical figure. Perhaps a better explanation of this phrase here is linkage with the next verse, where the verb *māṣā'* is repeated in the phrase, **the watchmen found me**.

3. The town **watchmen** reappear in fiercer guise in 5:7. Such characters feature prominently in similar love poetry in Arabic. In the Bible they appear in very different contexts: Ps. 127:1, 130:6 and Isa. 21:11f. Their reaction to a lone girl wandering scantily clad through the streets suggests "steely indifference" to Fox, particularly as they allow her to continue on her way in this passage (though not in 5:7). Gerleman suggests that such indifferent town watchmen are a recurrent theme of oriental love poetry: they certainly appear here in two different songs.

This passage probably refers to the town street patrols that grew up in the Maccabean period. However, Isa. 62:6, a passage which is probably earlier than this one, refers to "watchmen" set on Jerusalem's "walls", and Accadian texts refer to *sāhir dūri*, "one who goes round the wall" and *maṣar muši*, "night watchmen" (Pope).

As in 1:17, **him whom my soul loves** implies no particular psychological belief: **my soul** is used reflexively for the first person.

4. The importance of the adverb **Scarcely** (*kim'aṭ*) here is shown in the Heb. by its prominent position: it is in a clause of its own at the head of the sentence and is followed by the relative *šě-*. This can be represented in English similarly: "It was only scarcely after I had passed them that I found . . ." This unusual construction, with such heavy stress on the adverb, is discussed by J. Blau in *VT* 9 (1959), pp. 130–7: Blau even regards adverbs in such sentences as "psychological subjects or predicates". This takes things too far: it is sufficient to speak of short phrases being given particular emphasis by separation from main clauses.

Strangely, the watchmen are not credited with any reply to the girl's questions – perhaps she didn't wait! Such determination is certainly shown by the way she held him and **would not let him go** until she **had brought him** to her **mother's house** (this is the girl's desire in 8:2 also). Her **mother's house** is the natural home of an unmarried girl, as for Rebekah in Gen. 24:28 and for Ruth in Ru. 1:8, and also in at least one Egyptian song (Fox no. 32, p. 52). Such a straightforward Egyptian parallel makes it quite unnecessary to detect a euphemism for the girl's "welcoming" her lover "into her womb" (Goulder) – is not the womb the wrong part of the female anatomy, anyway?

5. This refrain, repeated from 2:7 (see comments there), seems to be used to mark the completion of this song concerning the girl's dream.

A ROYAL WEDDING?
3:6–11

There has been a great deal of scholarly disagreement over the meaning of this short poem. R. Gordis (*JBL* 63 (1944), pp. 263–70) notes that of the six references to Solomon by name in the whole book, three occur in this section (vv. 7, 9, 11). As for the other instances, the name appears in the title as part of the superscription (1:1), and in 1:5 (if **Solomon** is correct there, which we doubted when discussing that passage) as a generic title for rich curtains (i.e. like "Paisley" or "Liberty" material – Gordis suggests "Van Dyke's beard"); in 8:11–12 Solomon is cited as being famous for wealth, like Croesus of Lydia. But why does this poem mention Solomon three times? Gordis thinks that the name is authentic here and that we may have a genuine wedding epithalamium written specially for Solomon's marriage to a princess from foreign parts beyond the desert. On such a journey a princess would certainly be accompanied by a large retinue including an armed guard (though **sixty mighty men** (v. 7) seem rather a lot); the **column of smoke** (v. 6) may represent clouds of incense (with some poetic exaggeration). Gordis suggests that this is the oldest poem in the collection which was composed specially for Solomon's wedding in a genre similar to Ps. 45 which is a similar wedding hymn.

By contrast Gerleman sees here a description of a procession to and from the Theban necropolis in Egypt: the passage describes the annual Opet festival in which the god Amun would make a ceremonial visit to the temple at Luxor. The god was carried along in a procession from Karnak to Luxor by night with an armed escort. Certainly, the Song's links with Egyptian poetry are many, but Gerleman takes the Egyptian parallels too far here. The processional journey was only a few miles along the Nile valley (*not* across the desert), and much of the journey was made by boat (there is no mention of boats here) with armed escorts on the banks. This particular Egyptian parallel thus proves disappointing, particularly as the customs described above come from as early as the 18th dynasty (c. 15th and 14th centuries BC). Information on this festival and journey may be found in C. F. Nims, *Thebes of the Pharaohs* (Paul Elek, London, 1965), pp. 121–7, especially pp. 126f.

Rudolph accepts the passage as describing a wedding procession, since Solomon's wedding is mentioned in v. 11; but he notes several peculiarities. The poem never states explicitly who it is that is **coming up from the wilderness** in **the litter of Solomon** – is it bride or the groom? This vagueness leads him to suggest that the text is damaged and incomplete: he claims that a strophe is missing after v. 10. This lost piece of text must have described the bride sitting in a sedan chair or palanquin and the groom awaiting her at the bridal throne. This verse was omitted, he believes, when Jewish exegesis identified the palanquin with the holy ark, and its arrival with the ark's re-entry into Jerusalem after the exile: anonymous brides didn't fit such a scenario very well, so the verse was quietly dropped. The fact remains that no evidence for such a verse exists in the ancient versions, and we must therefore treat the text as it stands.

How are we, then, to interpret this passage? It would be splendid if the Egyptian songs described a young lover crossing the desert in his determination to reach his loved one – but, alas, no extant song seems to fit this formula. However, it is usually the boy who comes to the girl, who waits for him (cf. Fox no. 15 on p. 24); in one poem the girl imagines her lover coming to her swiftly "like a gazelle bounding over the desert" (Fox no. 40 on p. 66); in another the lover even wades through crocodile-infested floodwaters (Fox no. 20D on p. 32). So we can see that the lover is an heroic character in the Egyptian songs. We have noted a royal fiction used in 1:12f.; perhaps the poet takes the girl's romantic imagination that bit further, portraying it as being at fever pitch, surrounding her lover with all the trappings of royalty.

6. What is that . . . ? The words are intended as a rhetorical question rather than a request for information: the question is asked in order to draw the reader's attention more closely to what is being described. The identity of the one who is **coming up from the wilderness** has been discussed above at some length; however, some details need further comment. The Heb. words translated **What is that . . . ?** (*mî zō'ṯ*) would normally mean, "Who is this . . . ?", referring to a woman, as *zō'ṯ* is the feminine form of *zĕh*, "this". But in Heb. the feminine gender is sometimes used to denote the neuter (*G-K* § 122q), so *mî* may have a neuter sense, **What . . . ?**, like the Accadian *mi*. Lys tartly remarks that it is difficult to tell the sex of the chief traveller in a caravan at a distance – this is true, though you may have prior knowledge and be looking out for someone in particular (and this poem is a lover's fantasy, anyway). The Heb. *tîm*^{e}*rōṯ ʿāšān*, lit. "pillars of smoke", occurring also in Jl. 3:3, may, according to M. Dahood (*Orientalia* 46 (1977), p. 385), be derived from the Accadian *amaru*, "to see"; thus the Heb. could mean "signals", i.e. clouds of smoke or even of desert dust raised by the passing of a large caravan. If so, the original Heb. may have used the preposition *b*^{e}, "in" or "with", instead of *k*^{e}, "like", as these two consonants are frequently confused due to close similarity of shape in Heb. script. Thus Fox translates, "in columns of smoke". Lys notes that in Near-Eastern countries caravans were often preceded by torches providing light at night and smoke by day. At such a distance one could hardly detect the particular smells of **myrrh and frankincense** and **all the fragrant powders of the merchant**.

NEB translates: "(What is this coming up . . . like a column of smoke) from burning (myrrh or frankincense . . . ?)", revocalizing the participle **perfumed** (*m^e^qattĕrĕṯ*) as a construct noun preceded by the preposition *min* (hence *miqq^e^ṭōrĕṯ*): lit. "from the burning of myrrh and frankincense".

7. An unexpected grammatical construction appears in the Heb. here: in **the litter of Solomon** (*miṭṭāṯō šĕlliš^e^lōmōh*) the possessive suffix *-ō* is used with the particle *šĕ-* prefixed to the possessor. An alternative to the construct state, this usage is frequently used in Heb. from the Mishnah to the present day but is very rare in the OT. Such anticipation of a following genitive by a pronominal suffix was particularly common in Syriac and occurs earlier in Phoenician. Rudolph claims that the words, **Behold, it is the litter of Solomon**, are not required by the rhythm and were probably introduced later as a gloss on the strange word *'appiryon* ("palanquin") in v. 9. It is unwise to make definite decisions about usages in Heb. lyric poetry of the biblical period, as there is so little evidence; but such Aramaic-type constructions may have existed in early Heb. lyric poetry, to be taken up later in literary Aramaic and Syriac. This seems a better explanation than suggesting a gloss.

The lovers' royal fantasy develops further with **the litter of Solomon** and the **sixty mighty men . . . of Israel**. **sixty** is used here as a round number to denote "many", as also in 6:8. Multiples of six are often used in this way: for example, Samson has "thirty companions" in Jg. 14:11 and "about thirty-six men" are killed by the men of Ai in Jos. 7:8. The purpose here is to heighten the royal setting of the girl's dreaming. S. Krauss (*Occident and Orient, Gaster Anniversary Volume* (1936), pp. 323–30) suggests that the verse is concerned with the setting up a guard for warding off demons. He starts, not unreasonably, by asking why a royal personage should be afraid of the dark. He notes similar passages in early Jewish literature. Particularly relevant is the account in Tob. 3:7ff. of the experience of Tobiah's daughter, Sarah: she was married to seven successive husbands, each of whom was killed by the demon Asmodaeus on the wedding night before the marriage could be consummated. Krauss claims that the **mighty men** are groomsmen who guard the bridal chamber overnight against demons. This may take things too far, but certainly they are said to guard **against alarms by night** (v. 8).

8. The **alarms by night** mentioned here may be demons or evil spirits, as Krauss thought; but G. R. Driver doubted that the accompanying military gang would use **swords** to fend off such spiritual enemies. The verse stresses warlike rather than magical expertise. Though evil spirits may certainly have been rampant in the middle of the night, who can deny the likelihood of (very mortal) armed bandits raiding by night such a richly laden caravan going to a royal wedding? For **girt** the Heb. uses an idiomatic participle (*ʼaḥūzēy*), a passive form which was used later in Mishnaic Heb. to denote characteristics or habitual action. But *NEB* and *JB* may well be right in translating "skilled swordsmen", as the root in Accadian and Ugaritic denotes skill, cf. Accadian *'iḫzu*, "learning", *suḫaza*, "teach" and Ugaritic *'ḫd hrth*, "skilled in ploughing". **swords** occurs twice in this verse. J. Barr (*CPTOT*, p. 153) notes a possible pair of homonyms here: the Heb. *ḥereḇ* has been held to have two separate meanings – "war" and "sword" (it is noteworthy that the Arabic words *ḥarbu(n)*, "war", and *ḥarbatu(n)*, "javelin" or "lance" are very similar). Thus Pope translates: "All of them war-skilled (*ʼaḥūzēy ḥereḇ*) . . . each with his sword (*ḥarbō*) at his side", where the Heb. *ḥereḇ* is translated first as "war" and then as "sword". If so, the two meanings may be played off one against the other in paronomasia, as suggested by G. R. Driver (*VT* 4 (1954), p. 242). For **by night** the Heb. has a plural form (*balleylōṯ*): this does not imply experience over successive nights but rather fear of things prone to happen in the dark (like attacks by bandits or ghosts).

9. What exactly is the **palanquin** here? The Oxford English Dictionary describes a **palanquin** as "a covered litter or conveyance usually for one person, used in India and Eastern countries, consisting of a large box with wooden shutters like Venetian blinds, carried by four or six men by means of poles projecting before and behind." Such an Eastern link is quite possible: according to 1 Kg. 9:26 Solomon's fleet of ships based at Ezion-Geber on the Red Sea brought gold and precious woods from Ophir (probably in South Arabia, but possibly India). The importing of Eastern customs along with articles of trade is quite likely.

Scholars have disagreed quite fiercely over the derivation of the Heb. word here translated **palanquin** (*'appiryōn*). If the Song was composed sufficiently late to be affected by Greek influence, Jerome may have been right in suggesting (in his commentary on Isa. 7:14) derivation from the Greek *phoreion*, "sedan-chair" or "litter", a word found in Greek literature of the 4th century BC. But if such chairs were of Eastern origin, is not the Greek word itself likely to have come from the East – particularly as a similar word exists in Sanskrit (*paryanka*, "sedan-chair")? Both G. R. Driver and R. Gordis supported this link with Sanskrit; but others claim that the *k* in the Sanskrit word makes too many difficulties. G. Widengren suggested derivation from the Iranian *upari-yana*, a word which F. Rundgren (*ZAW* 74 (1962), pp. 70–72) rejected as non-existent. Gerleman prefers an Egyptian etymology, detecting a link with the Egyptian *pr*, "house": *pr-'*, or *per-'aa*, "great house" (the title of Pharaoh), preceded by a prosthetic aleph (cf. also T. O. Lambdin, *JAOS* 73 (1953), p. 153). He thus sees *'appiryōn* as *eine Thronhalle* ("a throne-room").

However we treat these details, this poem is certainly, to use Gerleman's term, a *Wunschsituation* (romantic pipe-dream) not unlike the royal fiction in 1:2–4 and 12–14. Gerleman prefers "throne-room" as a translation partly because he takes too seriously the list of rich furnishings that follows here (vv. 9–10). The **wood of Lebanon** represents the boards of cedar which Solomon used in building the temple (1 Kg. 6:15) and his own palace (1 Kg. 7:2f.). V. 10 says the **palanquin's posts** (pillars) are made of **silver**; **gold** and **purple** are used in the furnishings. On the basis of the meanings of related words in Jewish Aramaic, Fox translates "a canopied bed" – this is not a **palanquin** strictly, nor is it readily moveable. Goulder proposes "a vaulted throne", meaning a throne with a canopy supported by pillars (not unlike an enclosed but fixed sedan-chair?). He cites in support archaeological evidence from Tel Dan, where excavators have discovered the foundation of a throne with four stone bases for wooden columns which would have supported a canopy (cf. "Dan" in M. Avi-Yonah (ed.), *Encyclopaedia of Archaeological Excavations in the*

Holy Land, vol. I (Oxford, 1975), pp. 312ff.). Thus archaeological evidence seems to illustrate a structure similar to the one described here. (Goulder's archaeological evidence is better than his philological: to help explanation of the Heb. *'appiryōn* along these lines, he links the word to the Heb. *'apar*, "covering" or "bandage"; but this seems in a somewhat different class from a canopy, and does not help.)

How does all this fit **the litter of Solomon** which was **coming up from the wilderness** in v. 6? Not very well, if taken literally. Can a sedan-chair or a throne with a canopy be taken across the desert? But this is a lover's dream, and we should be asking how fair it is to take such a dream logically – we wouldn't today, I suspect! Human imagination switches images very quickly, particularly when roused by love and described in poetry. And poetry is what we have here.

10. The furnishings of the canopied throne are now described in luxurious terms that suit a lover's dream well. One can hardly imagine all this heavy **silver** and **gold** being carried over the desert, but in a lover's dream all is possible. The Heb. word for **its posts** (*'ammûḏāyw*) is more usually used of pillars (which suits Gerleman's throne-room well), but could also be used of the poles of a sedan-chair. Whether the **posts** here are solid **silver** or only overlaid with it hardly matters – this is a dream, and dreams transcend reality anyway.

The Heb. word for **its back** (*rᵉpîḏāṯō*) occurs only here: the Qal of the cognate verb is used in Job 41:30 of the crocodile spreading itself over mud like a threshing sledge and thus leaving marks on it; the Piel is used in Job 17:13 of making a bed and in Ca. 2:5 of refreshing (supporting? building up?) the sick girl with apples. Spreading and supporting (even metaphorically) seem to be the chief meanings of the root. For Gerleman this word denotes the gold-covered ceiling of the throne-room, supported by the pillars. There seems to be no reason why the term should not be used of the solid **back** of the seat, which in the dream is made of **gold**.

The actual **seat** itself would be of **purple** upholstery. The Heb. *'argāmān* is related to the Ugaritic *'rgmn* and the Accadian *argamannu*: it means cloth dyed a reddish purple, the dye being prepared from the shells of certain molluscs found on the Phoenician coast. This dye was much in demand for "royal" purple and was often required as tribute from the cities on that coast – indeed, the Ugaritic *'rgmn* is used in the sense of "tribute" (cf. M. Ellenbogen, *Foreign Words in the Old Testament* (1962), pp. 38f.).

RSV's **it was lovingly wrought within** is an attempt to make sense of the Heb. *tôḵō rāṣûp̱ 'ahᵃḇāh*, apparently "its interior was paved with love". The participle *rāṣûp̱* comes from a verb which is used only here and is related to *rispāh*, "pavement": like other terms in this verse *rāṣûp̱* is very material, and it seems wrong to lose this material sense in the vague **wrought**. But the interior can hardly be "paved" with non-material "love"! A noun denoting another material substance is needed. Some scholars have suggested that the text originally read *hŏḇnî*, "ebony"; but ebony is suitable only for the poles of an external framework. Moreover, reading "ebony" here requires quite a significant change of the Heb. text, the consonants of which are confirmed by nearly all the ancient versions. G. R. Driver (in *Festschrift für Alfred Bertholet* (1950), pp. 134f.) suggested a homonym: the Heb. *'ahᵃḇāh* could be related here to the Arabic *'ihabu(n)*, "skin, hide, leather", whence *NEB* has "its lining was of leather" (cf. *JBL* 55 (1936), p. 111), a meaning he finds also in Hos. 11:3–5 (cf. *JTS* 39 (1938), pp. 160ff.). For Goulder this makes yet another *double entendre* – a device which the Song's author often uses.

Are we then to imagine **the daughters of Jerusalem** (mentioned at the end of the verse) as workers in leather? Hardly! For this reason *NEB* holds them over to v. 11, where they make a good parallel to the daughters of Zion in that verse. Fox does the same thing in his translation. Furthermore, he attaches the *m* of *mibbᵉnōṯ* (**by the daughters of . . .**) as a plural ending (*-îm*) to *'ᵃḇānîm* ("stones"), which, he claims, was corrupted to *'ahᵃḇāh* ("love") through similarity of letters, especially *aleph* and *beth*. He then translates, "its [i.e. the canopied bed's] interior inlaid with stones". This is a clever emendation, as most of the requisite consonants are around – but would a canopied bed with a stony interior be very comfortable? I think it much more likely that the interior was made of leather dyed purple.

11. It is not clear why it is the **daughters of Zion** who are here exhorted to admiration rather than the more familiar **daughters of Jerusalem** – unless, as Fox suggests, they are introduced to balance the **daughters of Jerusalem** in poetic parallelism, a view which leads him to alter the division between vv. 10 and 11, as noted above. In either case **the daughters of Zion** are just stage figures, introduced as a suitable mouthpiece to express objective admiration of the two lovers: such description of beauty comes more naturally from some third party other than the poet himself.

The royal fiction for the lovers is continued and here extended to include **the crown with which his mother crowned him**. Wreaths are depicted in Egyptian paintings of banquets, and in one Egyptian love song (Fox no. 19 on p. 27) the girl accepts wreaths from her lover. Such a wreath could well turn into a crown in the girl's romantic imagination, which has already been seeing things through the eyes of royal fiction. Whether the giving of a crown was a special custom in weddings at that time we do not know. In Isa. 61:10 the "bridegroom decks himself with a garland" and the "bride adorns herself with jewels", but that is no evidence for gifts from the groom's **mother** as here. In later times crowns were worn by ordinary grooms and brides, but the custom ceased in 70 AD as a sign of mourning after the disastrous war against Rome (cf. Babylonian Talmud, *Sotah* 49a). It may well be that the custom of crowning the groom had a reasonably long history – perhaps it was an established tradition when the Song was written.

ADMIRATION OF THE BELOVED
4:1–7

This section is bracketed by vv. 1 and 7, where the lover makes very similar remarks of admiration for the girl – this is literary inclusion, as in 2:8–17. This poem is much more characteristic of the Arabic *waṣf* than the dialogue poem in 1:9–17 is: here the lover completes a typically detailed description of the girl's beauty and charms, starting with her eyes and hair in v. 1 and continuing down to her breasts in v. 5. The poem then concludes with expressions of his ardent desire and intentions. Wetzstein's association of the Song with Syrian marriages customs has led some interpreters to see these *waṣfs* as marriage songs (4:1–7, 1:9–17); but there is no evidence to support this, and the Egyptian songs which show such close parallels to the poems in the Song seem not to be linked with any particular ceremony. Such *waṣfs* were simply songs of erotic admiration, not linked with any specific *Sitz im Leben* ("setting in life"). Plentiful examples of this genre exist in modern Arabic poetry and, nearer the Song's date of origin, in the fulsome description of Sarah's beauty in the Aramaic *Genesis Apocryphon* found at Qumran. This whole genre is discussed by W. Herrmann in "Gedanke zur Geschichte des altorientalischen Beschreibungslied" in *ZAW* 75 (1963), pp. 176–97.

4:1. The *waṣf*, spoken by the lover, begins praise of the physical beauty of the girl with a general statement – **you are beautiful** – which is then repeated. Such repetition may be another example of the archaic stylistic trait noted in 2:15 (see the commentary there); however, it is more likely that the repetition is meant to portray the speaker's passionate excitement (as in 1:15, where the first seven words in the Heb. are identical with those here). This picture of the girl as veiled conflicts with 1:6, which said she was **swarthy, because the sun** had **scorched** her: the girl working (or slacking) in open fields under a scorching sun gives place to a more delicate, refined young lady whose dove-like eyes can only be glimpsed behind her veil. But this apparent inconsistency only reflects the Song's nature as a collection of different poems on roughly the same theme: the two girls are *not* the same (*pace* Goulder, who sees one developing plot) and belong to very different contexts. The poem in 1:5–8 used a rustic, garden setting; here we have a sophisticated description of feminine beauty.

For the significance of the dove imagery for the beloved's eyes, see the comments on 1:15. In that passage Gerleman explained the imagery with reference to the stylistic conventions of Egyptian art; in this passage he goes a good deal further, suggesting that the poet describes the beauty of the beloved as if she were a statue, using the rich imagery of Egyptian statuary to present the loved one's physical attributes in ideal terms. Thus here the plaits and ringlets of the hairstyles depicted in Egyptian art and portraiture have become in poetic fantasy **a flock of** [black] **goats, moving down the slopes of Gilead** – the girls' hair is flowing and rippling rather than tightly styled.

Gilead is the name of a locality on the edge of the Transjordanian plateau, home of the warlord Jephthah (cf. Jg. 11f.). The poet seems to describe the view eastwards from the western side of the Jordan valley.

The word *galᵉšu*, here translated **moving down**, presents a problem: it occurs only here and below in 6:5. *BDB* gives the meaning as "sit" or "sit up" or possibly "recline" on the basis of the Arabic *jalasa*, "sit up". This makes nonsense here, unless G. R. Driver was right in his theory of opposite meanings in some Arabic words: could **moving down** be a suitable opposite to the Arabic "sit"? J. Barr has a good discussion of this "opposites" phenomenon (*CPTOT*, pp. 173–7), but in this case he thinks the Arabic root of little help (p. 161). The ancient translations are not immediately helpful: LXX ("were revealed") and Symmachus ("appeared") seem to derive the word from *glh*, "reveal", rather than *glš*, and both Vulg. and Pesh. have "ascended" (*še'ālû*?). Whatever meaning is adopted, it must be suitable for both the beloved's hair and the flock of goats. Gerleman says, quite mistakenly, that the word occurs in Isa. 47:12, but it doesn't; he then suggests that a similar form appears in Egyptian texts, possibly as a Heb. loan-word, used of goats skipping or leaping. Skipping goats hardly resemble long hair, though they might do if they were skipping down a steep hillside in large numbers. Further, it is strange to suggest a Heb. loan-word in Egyptian from a text as unclear as this. The later Mishnaic verb means "bubble up", used of boiling water – quite the wrong connotation for animals coming down. G. R. Driver made two suggestions: from Pesh. and Vulg. he gleaned a possible "started up from (Mount Gilead)", but this doesn't fit the required comparison with hair. Pope adduces a usage of *glṯ* in Ugaritic with the cosmic ocean as its subject (that is water, at least!). This suggests to him the translation, "streamed", which can apply happily to both water and hair. Thus we may translate, "goats streaming down Mount Gilead".

2. The description moves down to the girl's **teeth**: most commentators, as *RSV*, take the sheep under comparison to be already **shorn**, but are we sure that the resultant skin colour would be white, like the colour of healthy **teeth**? *GNB* paraphrases "white as sheep"; **the washing** would presumably cleanse their white wool. Gordis sees gerundive force in the participle *haqq*ᵉ*ṣûḇōṯ*, "ready to be shorn"; i.e. the sheep are really white only immediately after **the washing**. *RSV* takes the second part of the verse as referring to the sheep, using the words **bear twins**; however, it is quite possible that the twinning refers to the **teeth**: the girl has full sets of upper and lower teeth with none missing. It is difficult to reproduce this double meaning. *GNB* throws in its lot quite definitely with the teeth: "not one of them is missing: they are all perfectly matched". *AB* perhaps comes nearest: "all of them twinning, none bereft among them". The second half of the verse seems awkwardly expressed: this is because the author sought to include an ingenious assonance between **all of which** (*šekkullām*) and **bereaved** (*šakkulāh*).

3. The comparison of the girl's **lips** to **a scarlet thread** is not surprising. All the comparisons so far in this *waṣf* are visual, emphasizing shapes and colour: **eyes** like **doves**, **hair** like a black **flock of goats**, **teeth** as white as **shorn ewes**. Egyptian women are known to have painted their lips to emphasize them – maybe to make them look thicker, as some suggest. Whether this description is based on a painting, as Gerleman suggests, or whether it represents merely an imagined portrait of an idealized young lady, looks and features are the main things depicted. So the girl's **lips** (which are distinctive in colour) are, like her **eyes** (which are distinctive in shape), seen even **behind** her **veil** (cf. v. 1).

The word for her **mouth** is unusual, occurring only here in the OT: the usual word for "mouth" is *peh*, occurring 485 times: here we have *miḏbārēyḵ*, the consonantal text implying a plural form (usually *-ăyiḵ*), the vowels a singular (*-ēḵ*). The ancient versions (LXX, Vulg., Pesh.) translated this unexpected word as "your speech"; but this is unlikely here in a list of physical features. Why, then, does this author use what appears to be an abstract noun (i.e. "your speech") instead of the usual *pîḵ*, "your mouth"? J. Barr (*CPTOT*, p. 147) suggested deliberate use of a homonym here. Fox, noting this as the only noun in a series of otherwise adjectival predications, detected a double pun (*VT* 33 (1983), p. 204): the usual meaning of *midbār* is "desert, wilderness", and *nā'wĕh*, **lovely**, is very similar (especially in sound) to *nāwĕh*, "habitation". Her mouth is thus cleverly portrayed as a fertile oasis with lovely words flowing out of it – not to mention possible heavy wet kissing.

Next come her **cheeks** (singular in Heb.), which are likened to **halves of a pomegranate**. As her cheeks lie **behind** her **veil**, the reference may be to the membranes in a pomegranate which separate the red seeds like a kind of webbing: so the features of the girl can be detected behind the "webbing" of the veil. But were veils of those days made with webbing? Were they diaphanous, or could one see the girl's features only when she raised her veil? I suspect the latter. Large veils were worn before the coming of Islam, as shown by R. de Vaux's detailed treatment of the topic in *RB* 44 (1933), pp. 397–412. Even if a girl's veil was only occasionally lifted, her lover could imagine the facial details of his beloved behind it, and his imagination would enhance them. But perhaps we take the imagery wrongly. Sensual imagery is not always visual: in 1:3 the imagery was of smell, in 2:3 of taste, and it may here be half of taste, half of sight. The contents of a halved pomegranate behind the hard rind are not only coloured a delightful red, but also taste sweet – thus we have a double appeal to the senses.

4. Long necks may have been considered graceful in Egypt, but the point of this comparison lies not in physical beauty – there are too many military weapons for that! **the tower of David** may have existed as a famous building, though we hear nothing of it elsewhere. The present tower of that name near the Jaffa gate in Jerusalem is more recent, dating originally from Herod. If the poet wished to describe a strong citadel, he might well add David's name to give it glory, as David was the military hero of Jerusalem. With David's name the tower becomes an impregnable citadel. The point here lies in the weapons hanging on the tower. We know of shields hung on battlements from Ezek. 27:11 and of others hung in the temple from 1 Mac. 4:57. The word translated here **for an arsenal** (*lᵉṯalpiyyoṯ*) is uncertain in meaning. The ancient translators adopted various solutions: Vulg. "with battlements", Symmachus "to a good height", and LXX gives up and transliterates! A. M. Honeyman suggested a possible solution (*JTS* 50 (1949), pp. 51ff.): deriving the word from a supposed root *lp'* similar in meaning to the Arabic *lafa'a*, "to arrange in courses", used of a building technique in which stones were laid in regular layers upwards, he showed that the point of the comparison was not the neck but the necklaces hanging round it, not unlike rows of shields on a tower. B. S. J. Isserlin (*PEQ* 90 (1958), pp. 59f.) took Honeyman's suggestion further, illustrating it with a photograph of a famous sculpture from Cyprus of a female figure wearing such a multiple necklace. *NEB*'s translation reflects this well: "(David's tower) which is built with winding courses". Isserlin's photograph makes this comparison plain: the girl wears several fine necklaces, one above the other.

5. A delicate pastoral image is created by this reference to **two fawns**. Gazelles are well known for their grace and sprightliness, and the author's intention is probably to ascribe these qualities to the girl. Goulder thinks the reference to the **fawns**, the foreheads of which slope steeply down to their delicate noses, is an allusion to the curve of the young woman's breasts, which slope down to their nipples – but this interpretation is less likely. Readers interested in the identity of the animals should read G. R. Driver's article in *Festschrift für Alfred Bertholet* (1950), pp. 135f. **that feed among the lilies** is omitted by some modern translations as introduced from 2:16; but the lilies may refer here to the scent of the girl's body, as the lover's lips are compared to lilies in 5:13. Goulder suggests that the phrase refers to the girl's breasts brushing against the hairs on the lover's chest. But this takes eroticism too far: the pastoral atmosphere of the love songs explains the phrase better.

6. The first half of this verse is identical with the first half of 2:17, where the commentary discussed the time of day when **the shadows flee**. The choice between morning and evening as suitable times for shadows fleeing is not entirely resolved here: the young lover may look forward to being with his beloved either at midday in a private place or in the evening and through the night to daybreak. Either is here possible. The important thing to notice is the second half of the *waṣf*: the young man has described the girl's beauty from her hair and eyes down to her breasts; then he says he **will hie** him **to the mountain of myrrh and the hill of frankincense**. It is difficult to avoid suggesting that the climax of his love is their intercourse, here expressed in imagery of hills and spices. Goulder is to that extent quite correct: sexual overtones can hardly be denied here. It is thus idle to seek a geographical location for **the mountain of myrrh** and **the hill of frankincense**. These spices don't grow in Israel, anyway; rather, they are costly perfumes imported from the East, like the **bag of myrrh** between the girl's breasts in 1:13. If the *waṣf* runs to a climax, that climax is here, even though the personal features of the girl's body seem drowned in costly perfume. Erotic smells were more fashionable then!

7. The poem closes with inclusion, repeating words from the beginning of v. 1. In *RSV* the effect of the inclusion is somewhat spoiled: the Heb. word *yāp̄āh* is used in both verses, but *RSV* renders it **beautiful** in v. 1 and **fair** here. Without repetition of the same English word, the effect is spoiled. However, v. 7 is not entirely a repetition of v. 1: **there is no flaw in you** is added to underline the girl's beauty just once more before the close.

AWAY TO THE DELIGHTS OF LOVE!
4:8–5:1

Commentators have found it difficult to divide off separate units in this passage, largely because at first sight the sections seem very broken up, though often linked by catchwords. Some have detected in 4:9–15 another *waṣf*, but on closer inspection the poem does not describe the physical features of the girl's body in detail as the *waṣf* in 4:1–7 does. Only her lips, tongue and eyes are mentioned; the rest of the poem deals in mountain peaks, orchards and, especially, gardens, spices and scents. H. Ringgren found here fragments of three different songs (4:8; 4:9–11; 4:12–5:1): v. 8 was originally separate; vv. 9–11 were planned as a direct continuation of v. 8; then 4:12–5:1 is held together as a unity by inclusion, with references to the beloved as the lover's garden at beginning and end.

But 4:8 is hardly a lone verse without relation to what follows. Fox has shown how this whole section is held together by literary devices like paronomasia, puns and repetitions – clear in the Heb. but not always clear in translation. The name of the mountain called **Lebanon** in 4:8, 11 and 15 is echoed in the sound of the Heb. word for **frankincense** (*l*ᵉ*ḇōnāh*) in 4:14; the **spice** (*b*ᵉ*sāmîm*) of 4:10 and 14 is echoed in **its fragrance** (*b*ᵉ*sāmāyw*) in 4:16. The **honey and milk** of 4:11 reappear in 5:1; similarly, **its choicest fruits** (*m*ᵉ*gāḏāyw*) in 4:16 recalls **with all choicest fruits** (*'im p*ᵉ*rî m*ᵉ*gāḏîm*) in 4:13. **my bride** (*kallāṯî*) in 4:8 and 11 links with **my sister, my bride** (*ᵃḥōṯî kallāh*) in 4:9, 10 and 12 and 5:1. Finally, the Heb. contains a clear play on words between the **lions** (*ᵃrāyōṯ*) of 4:8 and **I gather** (*'ārîṯî*) in 5:1. Such links underline the unity of the section.

This poem is a dialogue between the two lovers. The lover rapturously invites his beloved to come to him from the wild, mountainous, rural areas, using all kinds of flattering endearments (vv. 9–15) including spice and water imagery. The girl replies (v. 16) by inviting him to approach and enjoy love's delights. He does so, and the section finishes with some third party (the daughters of Jerusalem or the poet himself?) encouraging them to lose themselves in love.

8. The Heb. word for **with me** is understood differently by the ancient versions: Pesh. and Vulg. have "come" (*ᵉṯi*), LXX has "hither", probably reading the same imperative verb as Pesh. and Vulg. MT has **with me** (*'ittî*): the three versions read the same consonants but different vowels. *RSV* seems to reflect both verb and preposition in **Come with me** (*ᵉṯî ittî*). The recurrence of this phrase in the same verse illustrates the repetitive style of some of the oldest poetry in Israel, as noted above in 2:15.

Lebanon is the general name for the chain of very high mountains (up to 10,000 feet) which run parallel to the coast north of Israel. They lie on the western side of the Beqa' valley, facing Mt. **Senir** and Mt. **Hermon** on the eastern side of that valley. **Senir** is said in Dt. 3:9 to be the Amorite name for **Hermon** – probably both names together denote the whole range of the

Anti-Lebanon. **Hermon** is high enough to keep snow all the year round, as views from Tiberias on the Sea of Galilee show. These three names thus indicate the mountains on the northern horizon of Israel; they are high, rough and inaccessible and are possibly meant to be a deliberate contrast to the luxurious **mountain of myrrh** and **hill of frankincense** mentioned in v. 6. For further information on these mountains see M. Noth, *The Old Testament World* (4th edn.), pp. 59f. and Y. Ikada, "Hermon, Sirion and Senir", *Annual of the Japanese Biblical Institute* 4 (1978), pp. 32–44. The roughness of this mountainous location explains the presence of wild **lions** and **leopards**; there is no need to bring Adonis myths into the picture, as A. Bertholet does in *BZAW* 33 (1918), pp. 47–53.

9. The expression, **my sister, my bride** here and in 5:1 does not imply an incestuous relationship: brotherly and sisterly terms of address appear frequently in Egyptian and Mesopotamian love lyrics, denoting merely closeness of relationship and not the marriage of siblings. The term **bride** seems here to bear no connotation of marriage but stands rather as an emotionally charged term of affection.

The Heb. verb for **You have ravished my heart** (*libbaḇtî* and then *libbaḇtînî*) appears only here in the Bible; it is seemingly a denominative verb formed from *lēḇ*, "heart". Even in the ancient world there were differing ideas about its meaning (Vulg. "pierced", Symmachus "encouraged", Pesh. "strengthened"). A. Cohen (*AJSL* 40 (1924), pp. 174f.) noted that rabbinic writers cited an occurrence of this verb in the Mishnah (*Shabbath* V. 2: "rams may go out (on the sabbath with their sexual organs) strapped up (*lᵉḇûḇîn*)"), claiming a similar meaning for it in the Song: the Gemara even drew that sexual sense from this passage. In Arabic *labbaba* means "tie a rope round someone's neck, join, tie". In view of all this, "enchained" or (as *NEB*) "stolen" might be appropriate, as "chains" are used playfully of bonds of love. Further, in Mesopotamia "heart" frequently has a sexual sense, and "the rising of the heart" is used of male erection: may the word have this connotation here, possibly as a pun?

Whatever the exact nuance, the girl accomplishes this **with a glance of** her **eyes** (*bᵉ'ăḥăḏ mē'ēynĕyḵā*, lit. "with one of your eyes") – a difficult phrase because in the Heb., although **eyes** are feminine, the word "one" is a masculine construct ("one of"). Rudolph, too literally, calls this nonsense because she sees with two eyes, anyway! Others understand *'aḥaḏ* as a masculine noun, "unity". Fox notes that a bead of precious stones is termed an "eye" in Accadian, and suggests a pun here between the natural organ and the flash from **one jewel of** her **necklace**. In view of the parallelism in Heb. poetry of this period, I believe that here we have another word-play suggestive of both flashing glances between lovers and the flash of a bewitching stare (cf. "If looks could kill . . .").

10. This verse is reminiscent of 1:2 where, as here, Vulg. and LXX vocalize *dôḏăyīḵ*, **your love**, as *dăddăyīḵ*, "your breasts", showing the same consonantal text but using different vowel points. Here, as in 1:2, the girl's **love** is said to be **better . . . than wine**. In 1:3 her **anointing oils are fragrant**, and here **the fragrance** of her **oils** is **better . . . than any spice!**

11. No English translation can reproduce adequately the assonance of the Heb. underlying **Your lips distil nectar** (*nōp̄eṯ tiṭṭōp̄nah sip̄ṯōṯăyīḵ*). As noted above, this poem lacks the physical descriptions of a real *waṣf* like the poem in 4:1–7. In v. 3 it was the resemblance of the girl's **lips** to **a scarlet thread** that drew admiration; here those **lips distil nectar**. Perhaps the lover is imagining the lips' sweet taste from their lovely appearance, or experiencing their sweetness by kissing them. The poem goes on directly to speak of **honey and milk** lying **under** her **tongue**: the salivary glands lie under the tongue. It is, however, possible that sweetness of speech is intended. The parallels drawn from Egyptian lyrics by Fox contain, amid purely physical characteristics, the words: "sweet her lips (when) speaking: she has no excess of words" (p. 52 – there is some uncertainty over this reading, however); and on a deceased wife's tomb we read that she was "expert with (her) mouth, sweet in speech" (p. 350). So in Egyptian love poems sweetness was clearly used as a metaphor for pleasant conversation. Further, though we opted for feeling **under** the **tongue** in kissing, in Job 20:12 Job is said by Zophar to hide "sweet" wickedness "under his tongue", and Ps. 10:7 says that "under" a wicked man's "tongue are mischief and iniquity".

So both metaphorical and literal interpretations are possible.

Even her **garments** smell pleasant: **the scent of Lebanon** is mentioned also in Hos. 14:6, where Israel's "fragrance" is said to be "like Lebanon". Both here and in Hos. the reference is doubtless to the scent of cedars of Lebanon. The smell may be due to clothes being kept in cupboards of Lebanese cedar, but garments were also thought to have a smell of their own. For example, in Gen. 27:27, where Jacob wears Esau's garments, blind Isaac mistakes him for Esau because of "the smell of his garments", and blesses Jacob by mistake.

12. The imagery of the lover's speech now turns to the delights of a well-watered garden and stays with that topic until he triumphantly enters his garden in 5:1. Such gardens were far more common in the fertile Nile valley than amid the rocky hills of Palestine – which only makes the imagery more striking to the poet's Palestinian public. In Jer. 29:5 gardens are valued for the (vegetable) produce they yield, and the luxury of actually possessing a garden is illustrated by the conflict between Naboth and king Ahab over Naboth's vineyard (1 Kg. 21:1–19). Such a precious **garden** could well be kept **locked** – a good image for the beloved, whose charms were reserved for her lover only.

In the second part of the verse *RSV* changes the Heb. *găl*, "fountain", to *gan*, **garden**: most ancient versions and many modern translations do the same. With this emendation the two halves of the line start uniformly: **A garden locked**. The second *gan* was misread by MT, probably because of the fountain imagery at the end of this verse and in v. 15. Goulder keeps *gal* here, taking it as a "heap (of stones)" and detecting a reference to the girl's "mount of Venus"; but if that was ever the meaning of the text (which I doubt), the fact that all the ancient translations support **garden** suggests that it must have been censored out of the tradition long ago!

13. Your shoots was considered inappropriate by G. R. Driver, who said the lady wasn't a plant! As remarked above, this poem isn't a real *waṣf*: the only physical features mentioned in it are the lips and tongue in v. 11, and in v. 12 the poem moves into garden and fountain imagery. Various scholars have continued to see **Your shoots** as referring to a part of the woman's body, and have exercised considerable ingenuity in the search: H. H. Hirschberg (*VT* 11 (1961), pp. 379f.) suggested "Your vagina" on the basis of a cognate Arabic word; other suggestions range from "canals" (met. for "womb") and "grooves" to "javelins" (met. for the girl's breasts)! Even *NEB* thought this word referred to a part of the girl's body, reading *l^eḥāyăyīḵ*, "your two cheeks", for *š^elāḥăyīḵ*, **Your shoots;** but the poem has moved on from physical description. In any case, how can the girl's cheeks (only two!) be likened to a whole **orchard of pomegranates**?

Your shoots obviously fits the new garden metaphor well, and should not be maltreated to fit the *waṣf*-like descriptions of v. 11. Plants and shoots show life and activity in a garden – particularly in sun-drenched, hard-baked Palestinian earth. The poet thus expresses the beauty of the garden by stressing the budding of new shoots and the flowing of fresh water, whereas in the British climate we would probably try to achieve a similar effect by specifying the different colours of the flowers.

Henna with nard seems not to fit the context of this verse, though the list of spices in v. 14 begins with **nard**. *NEB* omitted the phrase, probably wisely, as a gloss from a scribe who felt that **henna** had been carelessly left out of the text.

14. Only a few of these spices are known to have grown in Palestine: most were imported at great cost from India or Arabia. This seems reasonable, however, as the poet is describing a garden of really exotic plants: it is in fact a phantasy garden matching the phantasy of love. **nard**, or spikenard, was imported from India; the Heb. word *nerd* is a loan-word from Sanskrit. So too is *kărkōm*, **saffron**, which possibly refers to a plant from India the root of which contains a yellowish-brown, quick-drying oil used for colouring; but it may refer to a type of ordinary Palestinian crocus. **calamus**, *qānĕh*, is probably a perennial native of Central Asia: Jeremiah (6:20) asks: "To what purpose does . . . sweet cane (*qānĕh*) (come) from a distant land?" **cinnamon** is native to parts of Asia, notably China (cf. J. T. Milik, *RB* 65 (1958), pp. 72f.). **frankincense** came from Arabia and the Somali coast, and **myrrh** trees were dug up and transported to Egypt from the land of Punt by queen Hatshepsut to be transplanted in the god Amon's garden. **aloes** were native to India and Indo-China. In Prov. 7:17 the harlot lays out every luxury to entice her man and perfumes her bed "with myrrh, aloes and cinnamon". These spices were thus clearly linked with love: this explains the long list here. It culminates in **all chief spices** – perhaps this phrase was intended to cover any which had been omitted by mistake. Interested readers will find a mine of information about the plants in Y. Felics' Heb. study, *The Song of Songs: Nature, Epic and Allegory* (Jerusalem, 1964).

15. After the list of plants we return to the garden itself and the water sustaining such fertility: the **fountain sealed** of v. 12 now returns in the **garden fountain** to round off the list by inclusion. **living water** is cool, refreshing, running water, here envisaged as **flowing** – but does it flow all the way **from Lebanon**? That name is mentioned here to indicate the quality, not the geographical source of the water: **Lebanon** is here used as a superlative expression denoting flowing water at its freshest and best.

16. Having described the delights of the garden, the poem now moves towards its climax. The girl commands the winds to **Blow** the scents of her garden – the scents of all the spices mentioned above – to her beloved to encourage him to **come . . . and eat its choicest fruits**. Note that the winds are asked to blow upon **my** (the girl's) **garden**; then, after the fragrance of that garden has been wafted abroad with the intention of drawing her lover to her, the garden becomes *his* garden – a subtle indication of the girl's surrender of herself to her lover. The locked garden of v. 12 is now opened to him. The specific mention of the **north wind** and the **south wind** has no particular significance, as in Isa. 43:6, where "the north" and "the south" are asked to give up the prophet's sons and daughters – presumably exiles from Palestine. In that passage some geographical reference is meant, "the north" and "the south" representing the distant extremes to which the exiles had been scattered. Here the **north wind** and the **south wind** are mentioned separately to provide the right balance and parallelism for the poetic line, while implying the meaning, "all winds": this is pure literary artistry. The possessive suffix in **its choicest fruits** (*m*^{e}*gaḏayw*) could equally well mean "*his* (choicest fruits)". In a context where the girl's garden has become **his garden**, it seems to me that Goulder is right to say that the garden's **choicest fruits** should similarly become "his choicest fruit". This translation would neatly parallel the transition to **his garden** earlier in the verse, and would skilfully lead up to 5:1, where the lover responds by entering and claiming his garden.

5:1. This verse comes as the climax of the whole section. Many of the sensual delights of the previous verses are taken up here: the **garden** from 4:12, the address to **my sister, my bride** from 4:9–10, **myrrh** and **spices** from 4:14 and **honey** and **milk** from 4:11. Thus the first and longer part of this verse serves to round off the topics mentioned throughout the poem, as the lover responds to the invitation which his beloved gave in 4:16: she is now *his* garden, no longer locked, and he comes to enjoy all the pleasures it/she offers. Everything in it is now his – note how in his speech the possessive adjective **my** occurs no fewer than eight times in one verse.

A problem arises over the tenses of the verbs: all the tenses in the Heb. are perfect ("I have come", "I have gathered", etc.). But the imperatives of the last few words of the verse (**Eat, O friends, and drink . . .**) hardly seem to make sense if the **honey** and the **wine** have already been consumed. For this reason *RSV* translates in the present tense in all cases, though perhaps we should understand **I come** as in the past – "I have come/arrived" – then the eating and drinking (probably figurative for sexual enjoyment) follow in the present, as *RSV* indicates. The problem lies with the Heb. tense system, which is quite different to the English one; the Heb. tenses are fewer in number than the tenses in English but have the same amount of work to do. The Heb. perfect may be used for any decisive action as if it had already happened, thus emphasizing the sense of certainty. Here the verbs may be in the perfect tense to reflect the lover's sense of achievement – he is anticipating what is about to happen. An unspecified third party then encourages the two lovers in their love, whence several modern versions translate *dōḏîm* as "(be drunk) with love" rather than the vocative **O lovers**. Honey in the **honeycomb** was very pure and costly. The connexion between the life of nature and sexual enjoyment is well illustrated in the Egyptian poems: cf. Fox's no. 4 (p. 10), where the girl, addressing her lover as "my little wolfcub", says, "your liquor is (your) lovemaking".

The third party which speaks the last couplet of this verse is possibly the daughters of Jerusalem, who are addressed in 2:7 and 3:5, although they are not named here. Gerleman thought the poet contributed these words from his own mouth, but this happens very rarely in the Song. The remark certainly finishes the poem neatly.

ANOTHER NOCTURNAL SEARCH
5:2–8

This passage bears a strong resemblance to the *paraclausithyron* in 2:8–17, but it differs in one important respect: whereas in the earlier poem the lovers had conversation, here none is possible because, although the girl hears her lover's voice outside the door, when she gets up and opens the door, he has gone. She then sets off to find him, but is herself found by the town watchmen, who maltreat her (after all, she is out alone, and it is the middle of the night). The section then closes with her appeal to the daughters of Jerusalem to find her lover for her (v. 8).

This gives the daughters of Jerusalem the chance to ask her what is so special about her lover (v. 9), and she replies with a *waṣf* which extols his beauty (vv. 10–16). We will treat vv. 9–16 as a separate section in order to avoid long unbroken blocks of commentary; but we should note how these two sections are linked more closely than those earlier in the book. After the *waṣf* the daughters of Jerusalem ask the girl where her lover has gone (6:1), and they are answered with the formula of mutual possession in 6:2–3. Thus we see how the different sections are loosely linked, with 5:9 related both to what precedes and to what follows.

In this *paraclausithyron* the lover's appearance reads like part of a dream sequence (cf. S. B. Freehof, *JQR* 39 (1948–9), pp. 397–402): the girl's panic over clothes and washing (v. 3), the careful preparation of her body with fragrant myrrh (v. 5), the horrid shock she receives on opening the door (v. 6), the episodic nature of the whole passage – all resemble vivid fragments of a dream. And it is not surprising if the watchmen do treat her as a prostitute – the girl's behaviour seems remarkably similar to that of the "adventuress with smooth words" standing on her street corner in Prov. 7:6–23. For more information on the classical form of the *paraclausithyron* readers should consult the introduction to 2:8–17.

2. I slept would be better expressed in a stative sense, "I was sleeping", as the Heb. words form a simple circumstantial clause. **my heart was awake** is also a circumstantial clause: she did not awake suddenly; rather, she tossed and turned in a half-awake state of anxiety. The use of the word **heart** in Heb. is different from its use in English: used of the physical organ, it can denote the seat of the will, and *AB* may be right to translate it here as "my mind".

Hark! (*qôl*): the Heb. uses the same construction here as in 2:18: the beloved's voice here (*qôl*) does not literally knock at the door, any more than it leapt over the mountains in that verse! Fox thinks the Heb. verb for **is knocking** (*dôpēq*) originally denoted pushing and may have here the metaphorical sense of "urge" or "entreat" – to knock would risk waking the whole family, he suggests. There are few such dangers with gentle knocking, one suspects, and in any case the muffled, romantic knock at the door may surely be an integral part of the *paraclausithyron*.

In a hot, dry climate **dew** very often provides the only moisture for the soil, and thus it is used to denote blessing and fertility in other contexts also; this is so in many passages of biblical poetry, cf. Gen. 27:28, Dt. 32:2, Ps. 133:3, Zech. 8:12, etc. Such a connotation makes little sense here, however. More apposite are passages in classical love poetry: Anacreon 3:10 pictures Love (personified) as begging for admittance and saying, "Do not fear; for I am drenched from wandering about in the moonlit night." The lover's wet **locks** here imply a long journey under cover of night rather than a cloudburst.

3. *RSV*'s translation of this verse is modest if not prudish, and doesn't make much sense. The straightforward answer to her question about putting on her garment is obvious: if she wants to admit her lover, she could throw something on easily enough!

This weak excuse is followed by one even weaker: **I had bathed my feet, how could I soil them?** If she was only admitting him for love and not going out, she wouldn't soil her feet anyway; besides, the thought of soiling them doesn't stop her wandering around the streets later, looking for him (vv. 6f.). Removal of her garment may mean more than preparation for sleep: J. P. Brown (*JSS* 25 (1980), p. 12) shows how removal of the tunic was seen as a symbol of sexuality, and cites this verse as showing how its removal could amount to an open invitation. He cites Herodotus (I. 8.3): "a woman puts off her modesty along with her tunic". The Heb. word here for **how** (*'ēyḵāḵāh*) is often used in songs of mourning and lamentation: here it may show petulant unwillingness or even teasing. *NEB* reflects this well: "must I put it on again?"

The Heb. word for **feet** is used occasionally as a euphemism for genitals: this explains several instances of apparently strange behaviour in the OT, such as Ruth uncovering Boaz's "feet" at night on the threshing floor (Ru. 3:3–9), Yahweh shaving the hair off the "feet" of the Assyrian king (Isa. 7:20) and David sending Uriah home to "wash" his "feet" (2 Sam. 11:8) after he, David, had had intercourse with Uriah's wife (by this scheme David evidently hoped to cover himself against being charged with causing Bathsheeba's pregnancy). In Dt. 28:57 the word is used also of female genital organs. If the beloved's **feet** here denote her genitals, we have another case of delicate *double entendre*.

4. *Double entendre* continues: the Heb. word for **hand** (*yāḏ*) is used for "phallus" at Ugarit and Qumran and also in Isa. 57:8, where *RSV* claims, "The meaning of the Hebrew is uncertain" and translates "nakedness". M. Delcor (*JSS* 12 (1967), pp. 230–40) shows that *yāḏ* can mean "penis", supporting this with a surprising amount of material, both archaeological and philological. L. Eslinger (*VT* 31 (1981), pp. 275ff.) takes the literal, sexual sense even further: not only is *yaḏ* the male penis, but *kappōṯ hamman'ūl* (v. 5, translated in *RSV* **the handles of the bolt**) is taken as part of the girl's genitals: thus in v. 4 we could have "coital intramission", Eslinger claims, with the female response. It is small wonder that the Song uses *double entendre* so much!

to the latch: the word here translated **latch** means basically "hole", and is preceded by the preposition *min*, usually "from". On any interpretation of the verse this presents a problem – whether it is describing the lover's hand feeling through a hole in the door or his penis penetrating the beloved's body – *min* presents a puzzle. Gordis' "withdrew his hand from the opening" hardly represents an action that would lead the girl to **open** to her beloved (v. 5). Pope thinks "in from outside" is the nuance, and this seems to be the best suggestion.

my heart was thrilled is certainly to be taken of emotional excitement, although the word for **heart** usually means "bowels". Physiological precision is impossible here. Translations try various images: *NIV* has a pounding heart; Fox has "my insides moaned"; *AB* has "my inwards seethed"; *NEB* has "my bowels stirred within me"; *JB* has "I trembled to the core of my being" – all choosing a phrase suitable to describe an extreme emotional experience. Such emotional states were expressed in ancient Heb. culture in frank terms which are difficult for us to understand and translate precisely.

5. In **I arose** the subject is specified by a personal pronoun separate from the verb (*ʾanī*). This is unusual in biblical Heb., as the subject pronoun is contained within the verbal form; it is stated separately only for emphasis, and no such emphasis seems intended here. Such pleonastic use of the subject pronoun is common in Ecclesiastes, whence some see in this usage evidence of a late date for the Song. However, such pleonastic usage appears in Ugaritic, Phoenician and the early Heb. of the Song of Deborah (Jg. 5:3). Pope therefore thinks the usage is a feature of dialect rather than of date. May it not be a feature of just that type of lyric poetry of which we have so few examples?

That the girl's **hands dripped with myrrh** is not surprising. The "wayward woman" in Prov. 7:17 perfumed her bed with myrrh ready for her lover. **myrrh** suggests more than just fragrant spices: in Fox's Egyptian poem no. 9 (pp. 16–17) the girl calls her lover "my lovely myrrh-anointed one", and the birds to be trapped (i.e. boys) are "anointed with myrrh" and have "claws full of balm". The girl here in the Song seems in preparation to have put on herself far too much sweet-smelling **liquid**

myrrh – so much that it drips **upon the handles of the bolt** (*'al kappōṯ hamman'ûl*) of the door. Eslinger (p. 276) finds here more *double entendre*: in view of his erotic interpretation of the beloved's **hand** in v. 4, he regards *kappōṯ hamman'ûl* as referring to various detailed parts of the female sexual regions, while the **myrrh** means the natural secretions of a woman in a state of sexual arousal. Even Pope finds this too much, and feels that Eslinger carries this "elaborate gynaecological conceit" to excess, thus detracting from the erotic intensity of the poem. But Pope judges this from the viewpoint of our modern ideas of sexual propriety, and we have so little extant ancient semitic erotic poetry that, in my view, we can hardly make such a judgement. If Eslinger is right – and he may be – these ancients may have been more explicit than we like to think. Even if **the handles of the bolt** represent the opening mechanism of the door, in a passage of such erotic content it seems not unreasonable to detect a *double entendre*.

6. In **I opened** we have another instance of the pleonastic use of the pronoun discussed in the commentary on v. 5. The Heb. for **had turned and gone** has two verbs in asyndeton, denoting a quick succession of actions: the construction vividly portrays the beloved's sense of sudden shock. This sense of shock is further expressed by the words, **My soul failed me** (*napšî yāṣā'*), the literal Heb. meaning of which is "my soul/life-force went out/departed". The same Heb. phrase is used in Gen. 35:18 of Rachel: "as her soul was departing, for she died"; there the meaning of the phrase is clearly explained as death. Fox suggests that the same nuance is intended here: "I almost died/collapsed in a faint". **when he spoke** (*b^edabbrô*) is strange: how did he speak if he had gone? His words in v. 2 can hardly be intended, as he left afterwards, and he now gives **no answer**. Fox revocalizes the Heb. consonants as *biḏ^eḇārô*, "because of him". I. Eitan, in *A Contribution to Hebrew Lexicography* (1934), pp. 34f., suggested a meaning for the root *DBR* from the Arabic *dubru(n)*, "back", and *'adbara*, "to follow someone". G. R. Driver took this up with his customary enthusiasm (*JTS* 31 (1929–30), pp. 284–5), and thus *NEB* translates: "(my heart sank) when he turned his back". *JB* and *AB* both adopt this translation. The final couplet of the verse recapitulates 3:2's "seek-and-find" theme; using the same words, it serves as a refrain.

7. The town **watchmen**, first seen in 3:3, now reappear, but in a slightly different role: there they seemed to be a kind of town police on patrol, but here the girl does not appeal to them for help – rather, they apprehend her, maltreat her in a way quite unsuitable for police, and take away her **mantle**. The only other biblical occurrence of the Heb. word for **mantle** (*r*^{e}*ḏîḏ*) is in the list of women's finery in Isa. 3:23, where it seems to mean a light cloak worn for special occasions with amulets, signet rings, etc. – certainly not the kind of garment for a girl to wear in a lonely search for her lover in the dark. Some scholars (e.g. Ringgren, Pope) have detected here traces of the famous Tammuz-Ishtar myth known from Sumerian and Accadian texts, where Ishtar seeks Tammuz in the underworld, losing her garments on the way. In the myths one ornament she wore is called a *dudittu*, a piece of jewellery given to her at her wedding; this appears on Mesopotamian figurines as a pendant. Pope suggested that the Heb. *r*^{e}*ḏiḏ* may have arisen from this *dudittu* through the frequent confusion of *d* and *r* in Heb. script. But no *d*^{e}*ḏiḏ* is known in Heb., and the meaning, **mantle**, for *r*^{e}*ḏiḏ* is supported by the Arabic *ridāt*, "cloak". If the Tammuz-Ishtar myth does appear here, it is only fragmentary, as Ringgren suggests, and has lost all religious connotations: it is used purely as a poetic motif.

8. As in 2:7 and 3:5, an adjuration to the **daughters of Jerusalem** closes the section. The similarity here to the other two passages is plain – even to the extent of addressing the daughters with the masculine form of **you** (*'eṯkem*) instead of the feminine. But this time there are notable differences. On the other occasions the daughters were adjured **by the gazelles or the hinds of the field**: this phrase is absent here, although LXX adds it (presumably to make this passage conform to the other two – an instinct for harmonization we have noticed before). The chief difference lies in the uses of *'im* and *māh*. In the other passages *'im* (frequently "if") is treated as part of the oath formula (cf. 2:7: **I adjure you . . . that you stir not up . . . love**) – a common usage of *'im*, including a negative sense within it without using the usual negative *lo'*. *RSV* here translates *'im* as the normal

if against the pattern of the other passages, where it is used as an oath formula: the passage thus becomes a simple request from the girl to the daughters of Jerusalem to tell her lover how sick with love she is. The word *māh* is taken as a rhetorical question: "What are you to tell him? That I am sick with love." This seems unnecessarily roundabout when the simple word for "that" (*kî*) could have been used. Fox (*VT* 33 (1983), pp. 204f.) takes *māh* in its less usual negative sense, like the Arabic *ma* (cf. *K-B*[3], p. 523), a sense appearing later in 8:4, where Fox translates "If you find my beloved, do not tell him that I am sick with love." What could be more natural than that she should be embarrassed about having run round the town at night half naked and that she should ask her friends not to tell her lover about it? And if readers feel that such sentiments wrongly presuppose modern society and ethics, let them read Fox's Egyptian poem no. 34 (pp. 53f.), where a girl in a complete panic says, "Don't let people say about me: This woman has collapsed out of love." Girls felt such embarrassment in Egypt long before the Song was written!

A LINK VERSE
5:9

9. It seems best to treat this verse on its own as a link between two sections. The words, **that you thus adjure us**, clearly look back to the adjuration to the daughters of Jerusalem at the beginning of v. 8. But the link with the preceding song does not rely on catchwords: the girl is here asked what she sees in her lover to make her behave in such a wild manner – wandering through the town at midnight half naked. This is not an unreasonable question to ask, and it fits the context perfectly, providing an excellent jumping-off point for the *waṣf* that follows (vv. 10–16) – the first *waṣf* to celebrate the beauty of the young man rather than that of the girl. It is unnecessary to see irony here: the verse gives a very taut reply to the lovesick maiden's pathetic cry in v. 8 for help in finding her lover, and the following *waṣf* comes very suitably to answer the question here posed. Such careful placing of the poems emphasizes the editor's skill in creating such a unified whole out of the poems to hand. Indeed, Goulder has argued for a "semi-unified sequence of fourteen scenes" leading "in a meaningful progression" from the girl's arrival at the royal court to "her acknowledgement by the king as his favourite queen". In my view Goulder makes too much of the "continuous sequence" idea. I do not detect such a continuous plot; rather, I see a loose concatenation of poems like the Egyptian collection. It is sufficient to show how cleverly and carefully the different songs have been placed together, with the link verses in between: it has all been effected most creatively.

ADMIRATION OF THE LOVER
5:10–16

In these verses we find another *waṣf* like those in 4:1–7 and 7:2–10; but, whereas those songs both celebrate the beauty of the girl, this one celebrates that of the man. This is unusual: love songs describing the physical beauty of a woman were not uncommon in the ancient Near East, but similarly detailed treatment of male beauty was rare. A passage similarly describing a man exists in Ugaritic (cf. P. C. Craigie, *Tyndale Bulletin* 22 (1971), pp. 11–15); although it is fragmentary, it can be seen that it follows the same descending order of description from head to feet. A song in praise of a man is found in Sir. 50, where Simon, son of Onias, is praised as high priest: much of the chapter is taken up with his practical achievements (vv. 2–4) and his magnificent appearance in the temple on the Day of Atonement (vv. 11–21). But in between we have a lyrical description comparing him to various natural features in a manner reminiscent of the Song's use of garden and nature imagery. This passage is not unlike a *waṣf*: indeed, we may say it has the same lyrical style as a *waṣf* does. But while Ben Sira describes general characteristics, the Song here describes parts of the body, from the head to the legs. Gerleman sees both this description and the *waṣf* in 4:1–7 as modelled on a statue. Perhaps Gerleman's theory has more justification here, as the man's features are described in material terms: his head is **the finest gold**, his arms are **rounded gold, set with jewels**, his body is **ivory work, encrusted with sapphires** and his legs are **alabaster columns, set upon bases of gold**. But the description is not wholly material, and there is mention of **wavy locks** of hair, **eyes . . . like doves** and **cheeks . . . like beds of spices**. So we may conclude that if the poet used the idealistic terms of statuary for his comparison, he did this only to a limited degree. Fox claims that in this imagery only the golden head is taken specifically from sculpture, "so we cannot suppose that the boy is being described as if he were a statue". It is likely that the poet was just drawing from artistic terms of comparison which were natural to him. Since later Arabic lyrics exhibit similar descriptions, we may be right in believing that this song belongs to a long-lived genre including ancient Egyptian and Ugaritic writings and Arabic literature.

10. The *waṣf* begins with a general description of the young man's beauty. The word **all** is not represented in the Heb., but has been added in the *RSV* to underline the general character of this verse, which precedes the detailed descriptions in vv. 11–16. **radiant** is a good rendering of *ṣaḥ*: this word is translated "clear (heat in sunshine)" in Isa. 18:4 and "hot (wind from the . . . desert)" in Jer. 4:11 – both passages are suggestive of the kind of shimmering heat which might be reflected off a statue (Gerleman). In Lam. 4:7 it is said of Zion's princes that they "are whiter than milk" (*ṣāḥû mēḥālāḇ*) – and they were no lifeless statues! If healthy bodies are thus described by a word from this root, then *ṣāḥ* may here mean "radiant health".

An adjective from the same root as **ruddy** (*'aḏmōnî*) is used of the youthful David in 1 Sam. 16:12 and 17:42, and a shining face is noted as a sign of good health in Ps. 104:15. Similarly, in Lam. 4:7 the bodies of princes are said to be "more ruddy [i.e. healthy-looking] than coral". This ruddiness was a good colour to have, and would mix well with sunburn. An additional purpose behind the use of **ruddy** (*'āḏōm*) here may be to suggest a pun with "man" (*'āḏām*).

Traditionally *dāḡûl* has been translated here **distinguished** or "conspicuous" (*AB*). G. R. Driver thought the term referred to someone or something being marked out, as with a banner (*deḡel*). But the Heb. *deḡel*, "banner", probably arose from the

Accadian *dagalu*, "to look at, see", already noted above on 2:4. So "admired" would seem a more suitable translation. *NEB*'s "a paradigm" takes it too far. **ten thousand** is not intended to be taken literally: that numeral is used to denote very large numbers, as in Ps. 3:6: "I am not afraid of ten thousands of people who have set themselves against me round about." In Ugaritic texts a myriad is used for a superlative degree.

11. Two Heb. nouns are used for **the finest gold**, apparently in hendiadis (*kĕṯĕm pāz*). The same two words balance each other in poetic parallelism in Isa. 13:12: "(I will make men more rare) than fine gold (*mĭppāz*), (and mankind) than the gold of Ophir (*mikkĕṯĕm 'ōp̄îr*)." In Dan. 10:5 the loins of the mystical human apparition are "girded with gold of Uphaz" (*bᵉḵĕṯĕm 'ûp̄āz*). The overlay on Solomon's throne is described as *zāhāḇ mûp̄āz*, "of finest gold", in 1 Kg. 10:18; in 2 Chr. 9:17 this is interpreted as *zāhāḇ ṭāhôr*, "pure gold". How far the words *Keṯem pāz* here indicate different kinds of gold we cannot tell; they may rather be used together deliberately in asyndetic hendiadis to emphasize the metal's richness, and it seems unnecessary to add "and" between the two words with LXX. Rich statues often bore heads of gold (an example of this is the shining image seen in a dream by Nebuchadnezzar in Dan. 2:32), but we need not therefore assume that this poet is here describing a statue. Homer describes Odysseus' head as golden without being accused of describing a statue. In any case, sunburn would have the same effect.

The word translated **wavy** (*taltallîm*) occurs only here, and has no plausible Heb. etymology. We may safely reject "hill on hill" as the literal meaning (i.e. the Heb. word involves a duplication of *tel*, "hill"), particularly as the cognate Accadian word, *taltallu*, means the stalk of the panicle of the date plant. According to Gordis some Arabic love poetry compares the beloved's hair to palm branches.

12. His eyes are like doves repeats a simile used twice before, in 1:15 and 4:1. However, here the simile is extended to include a fuller description: **beside springs of water**, etc. Goulder considered the image to be of the pupil of the eye bathing in the milk of the iris, but the colours don't fit well. The blue/brown of the iris could be said to bathe in the (white) milk of the surrounding eyeball; but it is more probable that the rest of the comparison, following on the **doves**, merely expands on the picture of the birds in their natural habitat (Fox) without illustrating the actual **eyes** any further. It is, however, surprising that the **eyes** take up twice as much space as any of the features mentioned in vv. 13–16. Rudolph may thus be right in suggesting that "His teeth" (*šinnāyw*) originally stood before **bathed in milk**: it is certainly odd that the teeth are omitted from this description, but the word appears in no ancient version. Certainly, the picture of doves bathing in milk is somewhat bizarre. Turbulent water is sometimes frothy and white as milk, but turbulent frothiness doesn't fit the context here: peaceful floating seems more the image required. "His teeth" (see Rudolph's suggestion above) would provide a reasonable feature for **bathed in milk** to describe, as healthy teeth are white. **fitly set**, as noted in the *RSV* footnote, translates the uncertain Heb. word *mill'ēṯ*, which is clearly linked in some way to the verb *mālē'*, "was full". If the teeth are referred to here, the expression perhaps describes two rows, a full set of teeth: we know from 4:2 that a full set of teeth was particularly admired – whence, perhaps, the phrase **fitly set**. However, if the imagery still concerns doves by water, we could translate "sitting by a brimming (i.e. full) pool". The Genesis Rabbah (Jewish Midrash) even suggests that the word *mill'ēṯ* means "pool" here.

13. The downward progression reaches the beloved's **cheeks** and **lips**. *RSV*'s **beds (of spices)** reads the plural form (*'arûgōṯ*) for the MT singular (*'arûgāṯ*, "bed") to agree with the plural **His cheeks** (*lᵉḥāyāyw*), thus making the two nouns, **cheeks** and **beds**, agree in number. This change follows ancient translations and involves no alteration of the consonantal text. Rudolph opts the other way, changing the plural **cheeks** to singular to agree with MT "bed", reading *lĕḥyō*, "his chin". Either way, we should ask whether what is described is the smell of his skin or the aromatic hairiness of his whiskers and beard; cf. Ps. 132:2, where "precious oil" runs down upon Aaron's beard, "running down on the collar of his robes". Would a young man sport a beard long enough to be compared to a plantation of aromatic trees (Goulder)? Perhaps he would in that culture!

yielding fragrance conceals another change to the vocalization of the MT. The Heb. reads for **yielding** a noun, *migdᵉlōṯ*, "towers", probably towers of perfume (Fox). This led Gerleman to think of the "towers" of spices, or more correctly the perfumed cones, which Egyptians wore on their heads at banquets (according to artistic representations). But this custom seems not to have been practised anywhere else but in Egypt, and the Egyptians did not describe these erections as "towers". *NEB* translates "chests full of perfumes", recalling the more modern use of the Heb. word for "(medicine) chests"; but it seems likely that this modern usage arose from this passage, where a *migdāl* or "tower" is said to hold spices. Vulg. has "gardens sown with unguents" or rather "paint-producing plants". LXX avoids the problem by revocalizing *migdᵉlōṯ* as a piel participle, *mᵉgaddᵉlōṯ*, lit. "causing to grow", whence *RSV*'s **yielding (fragrance)**.

The red colour of the lilies mentioned here gives way to **liquid myrrh** distilled in passionate kissing. The possible significance of the imagery of **liquid myrrh** in love-making was discussed on 5:5 above: here the reference is clearly to heavy kissing, where saliva "overflows" (one of the common meanings of the Heb. *ʿōḇēr*, here translated merely **liquid**).

14. This verse is full of terms suggesting statuary. *gᵉlîlē zāhāḇ* is here translated **rounded gold**, a rendering which weakens the simile. Apart from place-names, *gālîl* appears in the Bible on two other occasions: it is used in Est. 1:6 of curtain-rods, and in 1 Kg. 6:34 apparently of cylindrical pivots on a door. So, although the word here for **His arms** (*yādāyw*) usually means "hands", its rarer usage for the forearm seems more appropriate here: long arms resemble cylinders more than fingers do, and Fox's "his arms are cylinders of gold" seems to translate it well. The Heb. for **set**, *mᵉmullāʾîm*, a Pual (passive) participle from *mālēʾ*, "filled", seems strange at first sight: **set** (or even "filled") **with jewels** seems more appropriate for a ring-encrusted finger than for an arm. But that takes the root meaning too far: the Piel of this verb is used four times (Exod. 28:17; 31:5; 35:33; 39:10) in the technical sense of setting precious stones in the belt of the ephod, and the Pual used here is the regular passive of the Piel. **jewels** translates the Heb. *taršîš:* a precious stone of this name is unknown, though scholars suggest topaz, among other identifications. Gerleman, however, notes an ancient custom of naming precious stones from their place of origin: Tarshish was one of the ancient names of Spain, and jewels of particular kinds could have been imported from there, whence *JB*'s neat "jewels of Tarshish".

The Heb. *mē'ayw*, **His body**, is used of the external body rather than the internal intestines only here; the equivalent Aramaic word has the same meaning in Dan. 2:32. The Heb. word probably denotes the whole central part of the body. Uncertainty regarding its precise meaning increases our difficulties in correctly translating *'ěšeṯ šen*, **ivory work**. At Qumran the Copper Scroll (3Q15.i.5f. in *DJD* III (1962)) mentions *'astaṯ zāhāḇ*, "ingots, bars of gold", whence Gerleman suggests that this phrase could indicate an object of smooth ivory in form and shape resembling a bar of unworked metal. That **His body** should be compared to **ivory work** is no surprise, as classical authors quite often compared the colour of skin to that of ivory; cf. Od. VIII 156, where Homer describes Athene making the sleeping Penelope whiter than ivory. The **sapphires** mentioned here are not modern sapphires: the word was used in biblical times of lapis lazuli, as suggested in the *RSV* footnote.

15. His legs are alabaster columns: the Egyptian word for **alabaster**, *šš*, is clearly the origin of the Heb. word used here, *šēš*. Egyptian alabaster (calcite) is a crystalline, translucent form of calcium carbonate often used to make vases and ornaments. The young man's legs are here compared to it. Arab poets have compared girls' legs to pillars of white marble, so the simile here may be a traditional one. **bases of gold** probably refers to the plinth on which a statue was set, although Rudolph thinks the golden colour is that of sunburnt feet – but how then did the young man's white legs avoid sunburn if they were open to view? This may clinch Gerleman's view that the description of the young man is framed in terms of statuary. The Heb. word used here, *'ěḏěn*, is used also in Ex. 26:37 of "sockets" for the construction of the tabernacle, and in Job 38:6 of the earth's foundations.

His general physical **appearance** is likened to **Lebanon**, the huge mountain ridge described in 4:8. It hardly seems "hyperbolic" (so Pope) to compare a strong young man to such a mountain: it was the largest mountain around – and may not the point be that he is incomparable anyway? **Lebanon** is mentioned not only for its height and grandeur, but also for its luxurious **cedars** (cf. on 1:17). Famous for both imposing height and sweet-smelling trees, Lebanon seems an apt choice for comparison.

16. His speech is not a happy translation of *ḥiqqō*, although *JB* similarly translates "his conversation". The Heb. word here is used elsewhere in the OT of the physical organ of speech or of the palate, never of the word spoken. After this long, detailed physical description of the young man's body the literal translation is preferable: thus "palate" (Fox) or "mouth" (*AB*, *GNB*). Whether **most sweet** refers to the sweetness of **his speech** or to the sweetness of his kisses (as in 1:2 and 4:11) is uncertain, but these love poems seem more concerned with sensation than with what is said: so probably the words refer to sweet kissing. The Heb. word here, *mamtaqqîm*, comes from the same root as the Ugaritic *mtq*, used to indicate the sweetness of lips in kissing. Some commentators (Gerleman, Rudolph) feel that **His speech** (or even "His palate") is a poor parallel to **altogether** (*kullô*, lit. "all of him"), and emend *kullô* to read something more physical (*ḥinnô*, "his beauty"). This textual change may continue the sequence of physical characteristics, but it fails to reflect the climactic position of this phrase: at the end of the sequence "all of him" provides an important summing-up of the whole list, thus forming a suitable climax.

The *waṣf* proper thus closes with the first half of the verse, leaving the remaining words about **my beloved and . . . my friend** to echo the beginning of the section in v. 9. The song is thus brought to a close by literary inclusion.

ANOTHER LINK PASSAGE
6:1–3

This short passage links the *waṣf* describing the man (5:10–16) to the *waṣf* describing the girl (6:4–10). The questions in v. 1 are presumably asked by the ubiquitous daughters of Jerusalem, who again act as a chorus, as in 5:9. They are not specifically named in 6:1–3, but they are addressed in 5:16, and the questions in 6:1 follow on naturally. The editor has done his work well in arranging these two songs with this link in between.

In v. 2 we find a statement to the effect that the lover has claimed his beloved: this introduces his rapturous description of her in vv. 4–10. In v. 3 we have a formula of mutual possession very similar to that used in 2:16, except that the two nominal clauses in the first half-line have exchanged positions. The passage forms a neat transition between the two longer poems. Its original independence from 5:2–8 is clearly shown by the fact that there the girl does not know where her lover is (5:6), whereas here she is confident of finding him (v. 2).

6:1. The daughters of Jerusalem ask a question that prompts the beloved's statement in v. 2. This question illustrates the editor's skill in using such small links to weave the song collection into a whole (cf. 5:9). Here, however, there is more than a simple link: the words, **that we may seek him with you** attribute to the daughters of Jerusalem an additional motive. Usually passive, they apparently here wish to take an active part in the love affair – to interfere, in fact. Commentators seem not to notice this intriguing phrase. But, if vv. 1–3 are taken as a unit, vv. 2 and 3 may seem to answer both parts of this verse: the beloved states that her lover **has gone down to his garden** (v. 2) in order to pasture **his flock among the lilies** (v. 3).

2. As in 4:16 and 5:1, the beloved is the lover's **garden**, a symbol that suggests all the aromas and **spices** common to ancient Egyptian love poetry as to the Song; clearly the **garden** is an image comprehending all the girl's charms. It is unnecessary to lay emphasis on the lover's going down to the garden: Wittekindt and others have seen here a reference to going down to the underworld. Nothing here suggests such a veiled allusion to a *descensus ad inferos*, although Pope does cite passages from a hymn to Ishtar which describe plant life in the nether world. Gardens are said to have adjoined most rich houses in ancient Egypt, and contained lilies and spices. Such gardens would naturally have been near water, and on a lower level than living accommodation, particularly where river water was likely to flood. In any case, the Egyptians are said to have lived customarily on the first floors of their houses, so they would have been obliged to "go down" to get to their gardens.

In the phrase, **in the gardens** the plural seems strange, although it is present in MT and in the ancient versions. Gerleman claims that such a "generalising plural" should not surprise us in formal poetry – particularly as the plural is used in such a way in Egyptian poems. G. R. Driver cited an ancient form of personal suffix, *-āmō*, here "his (garden)" (cf. *G-K* § 91f.), which later scribes misread as the plural form *-îm*. This may be preferable to assuming a plural of composition reflecting the number of flowerbeds. *NEB* and *GNB* both read the singular form without further ado.

3. The strangeness of pasturing one's **flock among the lilies** has already been remarked on in the commentary on 2:16. However, this verse is not an exact duplicate of that passage: the two nominal clauses in the first half of 2:16 are here reversed. Joüon and Robert saw significance in this change: the girl here stresses that she now belongs to her husband and condemns her past infidelity – thus the first person pronoun comes first for emphasis. Rudolph thought that **his flock among the lilies**, though making suitable sense in 2:16, was inappropriate here: it seems unlikely for the man to pasture his flock among lilies when he has gathered lilies only in the previous verse! Rudolph thus suggests that the original participle was *hārōṣěh*, "he enjoys", and that this was changed to MT's *hārō'ěh*, "he pastures, feeds", to make this passage match the similar one in 2:16. This change would have involved only confusion of the Heb. consonants *ṣ* and ', a mistake which is easily made. Rudolph may be right. In any case, pasturing flocks among lilies is entirely unrealistic, fitting the sophistication of lyric poetry rather than pastoral reality.

LESS FULSOME ADMIRATION
6:4–7

After the brief link passage we find another song of admiration (*waṣf*), addressed to the girl by her lover. When compared to the similar *waṣf* in 4:1–7 it seems strangely weak, and falls away markedly after some very striking images at the start: hair, teeth and cheeks are common to both *waṣfs*, but lips, neck and breasts are here omitted. Furthermore, after the arresting descriptions in v. 4 and the first half of v. 5, hair, teeth and cheeks are described in exactly the same words as in the earlier song – except for the **flock of ewes**, which is not here described as shorn. But the general pattern is the same: a declaration of the girl's beauty (v. 4, cf. 4:1) is followed by a description of her eyes (v. 5, cf. 4:1), after which the wording is almost exactly identical to that of 4:1–3. But at the end of v. 7 the *waṣf* stops abruptly with the cheeks – Gerleman calls it a mere torso of a *waṣf*! There is a strange inconsistency in this passage: why should the girl be asked to turn her eyes away from her lover (v. 5), when she is wearing a veil anyway (v. 7)?

Such heavy borrowing and inconsistency suggest that here we see the results of editing which is later and less skilful than that which we encounter in earlier parts of the book. Gordis, basing his argument largely on the mention of Tirzah in v. 4 (on which see below), held that this song must emanate from the period when Tirzah was still the capital of the northern kingdom – i.e. the period between Jeroboam I (922–901) and Omri (876–869), the king who built the new capital, Samaria (1 Kg. 16:24). Such an early date doesn't fit the clearly secondary nature of the passage. Moreover, mention of place-names in lyric poetry does not provide evidence of date, particularly as names live on in memory and are sometimes cited to create a play on words, as seems likely here.

4. Tirzah was the capital city of Israel, the northern kingdom, before Omri built Samaria: it is probably to be identified with Tel el-Far'a, 7 miles north of Nablus. The excavations are described by U. Jochims (*ZDPV* 76 (1960), pp. 73–96). According to J. Gray (*PEQ* 1952, pp. 110–13) there was little grand architecture on the site, and this has been held to count against the identification. But, as Gray points out, the lack of grand buildings may well have been the impetus behind Omri's seeking to create a "real" capital city at Samaria. Although mention of **Jerusalem** in the same verse encourages us to find the capitals of the northern and southern kingdoms balancing each other in poetic parallelism, the ancient translators omitted the place-name: LXX "a desirable thing", Vulg. "pleasant, agreeable", Pesh. "as a thing of delight". Pope detected here an asseverative particle, *k*, borrowed from Ugaritic, and translated "(Fair you are, my darling,) verily pleasing": his translation then continues, "beautiful as Jerusalem", taking *k* this time as the more normal "like" – thus ruining his point, since in poetic parallelism an author would hardly use such a simple particle in different senses in two halves of the same verse.

terrible as an army with banners follows Vulg.'s translation (*terribilis*): such a comparison for one's beloved seems unlikely in any culture! Gordis (in his commentary and in *JBL* 88 (1969), pp. 203f.) suggested reading *'ēymāh k*^{e}*migd*^{e}*lōṯ*, "awe-inspiring with its towers" – a suitable compliment for Jerusalem; but he later kept MT *k*^{e}*niḏgālōṯ*, linking it with the Accadian *dagâlu* (cf. on 5:10), translating more simply, "awe-inspiring like these great sights", with reference to Tirzah and Jerusalem just mentioned; no textual change would then be needed. Gerleman approves the link with the Accadian *dagâlu*, but translates *die (nur) Gesehene* ("things (only) seen"): this refers, he claims, to mirages, things seen which do not exist. In Arabic literature such mirages are termed the *fata morgana*, and are frequently used in poetry for almost proverbial pictures of the unattainable and deceptive (German: *Trugbilde*). This phenomenon was described by the Greek author Diodorus Siculus in the first century BC as "something amazing"; he then goes on to describe the stunning effect of such visions on the people who experience them. "Awe-inspiring" certainly seems more in keeping with a lover's feelings of admiration than *RSV*'s **terrible**. The most acceptable solution seems to be that of S. D. Goitein (*JSS* 10 (1965), pp. 220f.), who notes that in both French and Arabic words meaning "awe-inspiring" undergo a semantic shift through "terrific" to "extraordinary". Further, he notes that *k*^{e}*nidgālōṯ* occurs again in v. 10 of this chapter, where it is parallel to **the dawn**, **the moon** and **the sun**. On the basis of the Accadian *dagâlu*, "to see", *dāgûl*, "distinguished", in 5:10 and the parallel heavenly bodies in 6:10, he suggests that *niḏgālōṯ* here are "things seen", i.e. "heavenly phenomena", and translates, "splendid as the brilliant stars" – as good a solution as any other!

5. The strange power of the eye to unnerve people was mentioned in 4:9, where the girl ravishes the young man's heart **with a glance of** her **eyes**. The use of the imagery there is more complex than in this passage. Here there is no suggestion that there is semi-magical, bewitching power behind a sharp, intent glance: the lovers simply look at each other with fondness. Such fond glances between lovers may be said to be disturbing, without any hint of a bewitching stare. In either case, eyes are recognized as useful, positive weapons: in 4:9 they are bewitching and frightening, while here they disturb the emotions with loving glances. A less threatening *double entendre* may, however, exist: L. Kopf, in *VT* 9 (1959), pp. 273–6, claimed that the Arabic verb *rāʿa* can mean both "alarm, frighten" and "awaken pleasure" (cf. also *VT* 8 (1958), p. 203). If such a double meaning in Arabic is genuine, similar semantic duality may be found here, he claims: her eyes **disturb** and unsettle, but at the same time give pleasure.

In the second half of the verse the Heb. wording is identical to that in the second half of 4:1, apart from the definite article before **Gilead**, which is present here but is omitted in 4:1. Some Heb. MSS, LXX and some modern editors omit the article here to make this passage conform to the earlier one. The overall similarity of the two passages perhaps justifies this, but in Heb. place-names do sometimes have the definite article, as sometimes in English (cf. the Cairngorms). But either way, it makes no real difference to the meaning of the Heb. here.

The wording of the first half of the verse is quite different from that of the first half of 4:1, but then **Your hair is like a flock of goats . . .** repeats exactly the wording of the second half of 4:1: readers should consult the notes on that passage.

6. This verse is very similar to 4:2, and for comments on subject-matter readers should consult the commentary on that passage. However, although the two passages are so alike, there are some differences. In 4:2 *RSV*'s **shorn ewes** translates the Heb. *haqqᵉṣûḇōṯ*, lit. **shorn**, the **ewes** being implied by the feminine ending *-ōṯ*; here the **ewes** are mentioned explicitly (*hārᵉḥēlîm* – a feminine noun with an unusual masculine ending) with no word of the shearing. In the ancient versions the same words are used on each occasion except in the Vulg., where Jerome accurately writes *tonsarum*, "shorn", in 4:2 and *ovium*, "sheep", here, following his policy of conforming exactly to the *Hebraica veritas*.

In the second half of this verse the Heb. is identical with that in 4:2, apart from the suffix *-am* here (in *šakkûlām*, **bereaved**) for the simple *šakkûlāh* in 4:2 – a seemingly minor difference. Yet *RSV* introduces two small changes where the Heb. is identical: **all of which** in 4:2 becomes here **all of them**, and **not one among them** in 4:2 is preceded here by **and**. These are very small differences, certainly, but why have the *RSV* translators introduced such arbitrary changes in translating the same Heb. words?

7. The Heb. of this verse is exactly the same as that of the second half of 4:3, and *RSV* corresponds exactly also. But there the couplet on the girl's cheeks was preceded by one on her lips and mouth: the omission of this couplet here has not been satisfactorily explained. Of the ancient versions LXX, Symmachus and Aquila all add the missing couplet after v. 6, as does Fox, thus assimilating this passage to its parallel in 4:3. But, as noted in the introduction to this section, this particular *waṣf* tails off badly after the fine language and imagery of vv. 4 and 5. Perhaps the original couplets following vv. 4 and 5 were lost, and later scribes tried to complete the description by repeating some items from the earlier poem – with rather colourless results: these verses are second-hand, and they look like it!

THE INCOMPARABLE ONE
6:8–10

It is a moot point whether this small section of three verses belongs to the preceding *waṣf* in 6:4–7 or not. Certainly, the reference to the girl as **terrible as an army with banners** in v. 10 repeats the words used in 6:4; this might suggest that here we have a single song, concluding at v. 10 with an inclusion. But that would make a single song of very uneven quality. We have already noted how the *waṣf* in vv. 4–7 loses its literary quality when, from the middle of v. 5 onwards, it starts tamely to repeat parts of the preceding poem in 4:1–3. One single song would hardly deteriorate suddenly like that and then suddenly recover its quality again in vv. 8–10. It is thus more likely that the compiler placed this fragment at the end of the preceding (possibly incomplete?) *waṣf* to provide some kind of fitting climax: he may indeed quite consciously have repeated in v. 10 the words **terrible as an army with banners** from v. 4 to bind the two poems together.

The motif behind vv. 8 and 9 is clearly the incomparability of the one girl among many women – a fresh feature successfully brightening up the ailing *waṣf* before it. The passage then culminates in the declaration of v. 10, with its astronomical imagery. As in the *fata margana* of 6:4 and in the *waṣf*-like description of high priest Simon in Sir. 50:1–21, in ancient Egyptian love poetry and in the Arabic *A Thousand and One Nights* astral, heavenly phenomena are used to enhance the beauty of a girl's appearance. Thus in this brief poem we have two motifs which serve to emphasize the girl's beauty and to bring the description in vv. 4–10 to a climax.

8. The number of women in the harem here deliberately emphasizes the one and only beloved mentioned in the next verse. The figures are notably more reasonable than Solomon's "seven hundred wives, princesses and three hundred concubines" in 1 Kg. 11:3. Rehoboam had a harem of more manageable size: "eighteen wives and sixty concubines" (2 Chr. 11:21). A king's historical significance was sometimes assessed by the size of his harem! We are clearly back with the royal travesty again. But it does seem strange that this fictional Solomon is not dignified with a harem anywhere near as large as that of the real king Solomon. This is possibly due to independent authorship: the Bible is not as full of cross-references as some people think. However, round figures in tens are rarely intended to be exact; rather, they simply indicate large numbers. Significantly similar gradations are noted in Ugaritic literature by W. F. Albright ("Archaic Survivals in the Text of Canticles", *Hebrew and Semitic Studies presented to G. R. Driver*, p. 1), who finds well-attested examples in Hurro-Hittite literature also. The **queens** here are not reigning monarchs or even the honoured wives of a monarch – even Esther is called a "queen" (Est. 5:2f., 12 etc.), although she was probably little more than one girl in a large harem. Regular wives are probably meant here, as distinct from secondary wives or concubines. The **maidens without number** represent a third class – probably prostitutes, as in Ugaritic texts the same word as the Heb. here (*'lymt'*) is used for "prostitute" (cf. A. Schoors, *VT* 21 (1971), pp. 503–5). But the whole point of this verse is to emphasize the incomparability of the one and only beloved in the next verse: such praise for a beloved is a familiar theme in the love poetry of all times and cultures, and needs no illustration.

9. The incomparability motif continues, but is now strengthened: after the high numbers of the previous verse the beloved is now said to be **only one**. This translates the Heb. *'aḥaṯ hî'*, where the predicate **one** is placed before the pronoun *hî'* for emphasis (lit. "one is she"). **only** is not literally represented in the Heb. text, but is a suitable way of representing in English the force of this Heb. emphatic construction: *AB* and *JB* both translate "unique". The Heb. *'aḥaṯ hî'* is repeated to give even greater emphasis (lit. "(only) one is she to her mother"), but *RSV* translates this second occurrence as **the darling of her mother**. The phrase is paralleled almost word for word in one of Fox's Egyptian love songs (no. 31 on p. 52), where a young lover exclaims: "One alone is (my) sister, having no peer." The root of *bārāh*, here translated **flawless**, suggests both "chosen" and "pure", both qualities of the girl's beauty: *NEB*'s "devoted" introduces an element of will and intention foreign to the Heb. here, where physical beauty is intended. Mention of the mother's love emphasizes further the uniquely precious nature of the beloved.

The phrases, **and called her happy** and **and they praised her**, are the only examples in the book of the *waw*-consecutive construction which is used regularly in biblical Heb. for prose narrative, where one thing happens after another in succession: the verb comes first and is linked to the previous clause by a particularly strengthened form of the conjuction **and** (*w*^{e}) (cf. *G-K* § 49). In view of the late character of the book's language, Fox suggests that the poet is consciously archaizing, using this narrative construction to introduce the women's words of praise in v. 10, which follow naturally on the lover's exclamation in this verse. This may be true: the poet needs to introduce the maidens' comments somehow. He wishes to show they are contingent on the lover's declaration and so he uses the *waw*-consecutive construction, which is much neater than inserting an extremely unpoetic "and they said". **the queens and concubines** clearly form part of the royal travesty, which appears from time to time throughout the whole collection. Their admiring words follow in the next verse.

10. The admiring words of the maidens, queens and concubines – the women of the harem – are now quoted. The words, **Who is this . . . ?** hardly pose a real question: they form here a rhetorical question expressing surprised admiration, as shown by the intensifying string of epithets in the rest of the verse, rising from dawn to sun and moon and then, probably, to a mirage (see below). Such questions are often used in daily life to greet admiringly someone dressed up for a special occasion. Similar questions are asked in 3:6 and 8:5. The Heb. word translated **that looks forth** has a clear connotation of looking downwards – from windows and the like: Rudolph claims it is an astronomical term. This certainly fits the epithets that follow: the moon, the sun and the astronomical apparition known as the *fata morgana*. As in 6:4 (see notes there), the latter is probably intended by the Heb. *kannidgālōt*, translated in *RSV* **as an army with banners** in both places. *NEB* translates, "majestic as the starry heavens". Comparison of a beautiful maiden with the moon is a stereotype of the Arabic *A Thousand and One Nights*, and similar comparisons are used of Simon the high priest in Sir. 50:5–7 and also in Theocritus' Greek lyric poetry. There is thus no suggestion that the girl is a goddess.

Curiously, the Egyptian love song which was quoted with reference to v. 9 (Fox, no. 31) continues in the same way: after the words cited above it compares the girl's beauty with astronomical wonders: "Behold her, like Sothis rising at the beginning of a good year: shining, precious, white of skin . . ." Sothis was the star Sirius, whose rising was reckoned to coincide with the rising of the Nile; thus Sothis was believed to bring fertility to the land.

ANOTHER LINK PASSAGE
6:11–13

The unskilful editing evident in 6:4–7 reappears here, and any decision over the significant placing of these three verses must remain uncertain – they hardly seem to fit! The words of admiration in 6:10 round off the previous poem very neatly; but the statement that someone **went down to the nut orchard** to inspect the vines and pomegranates clearly doesn't continue the preceding praise poem or follow on, even in the conventions of Egyptian love poetry. Equally clearly, another *waṣf* starts in 7:1, again admiring the girl's beauty. The references in v. 13 to the return and dancing of the Shulammite girl (if that is what the verse really means – see commentary below) serve well to introduce the *waṣf* that follows. Indeed, the question asked at the end of v. 13 comes very aptly before the *waṣf* in 7:1ff., which appears to answer it quite naturally. The editor may have composed these link passages himself to bind the different poems together more, but it is more likely that they were just fragments of very short poems which he fitted in with the rest.

As it is, these three verses appear isolated. Problems of text and interpretation in vv. 12 and 13 are considerable, making it impossible to see how these verses originally fitted into the sequence of poems. Verses 11 and 12 are linked by the use of the first person singular – are we then to assume that this is the same person who addresses the Shulammite girl in v. 13? If so, why does the **I** of vv. 11–12 become **we** in v. 13? Who is this **I**, anyway? In 2:10–14 it was the lover who invited his beloved to go and seek flowers and fruit: would *he* ever dream of being **in a chariot beside** his **prince** (if that is what the obscure v. 12 means)? The royal fiction followed elsewhere would suggest that the prince was the male lover and that it was the rustic girl who dreamt of being at his side. In that case the subject of vv. 11–12 is the girl; v. 13 is probably spoken by some third party or parties (a chorus?), like 1:4 or the last part of 5:1. The nuts, vines and pomegranates of v. 11 certainly relate well to the rustic fiction which we see in other parts of the Song.

So, although these verses seem to be composed of odds and

ends with no solid context in which to solve difficulties, they show clearly the marks of the ethos that pervades the whole book.

11. The first half of this uneven section opens with the maiden's account of her springtime trip to an idyllic garden. The frequent use of garden imagery in ancient erotic poetry to suggest sexual enjoyment has led some commentators to think this verse should be interpreted as the girl's response to the lover's invitation expressed in 2:10. But the poems are probably not integrated into a whole to that extent (*pace* Goulder): if they were, the girl would already have found her lover in 3:4 and would already have lost him when she wandered through the town in 5:5–7. Gardens are used in the Song to symbolize sexual enjoyment (cf. 4:12–16; 5:1–6:2), but it should be particularly noted that this garden is a **nut orchard**. The Heb. word for **nut** (**gōz*) occurs only here in the Bible, but is frequent in the Talmud, especially in discussion of this verse. In Jewish exegesis the nut garden becomes a symbol of the second temple in Jerusalem, but a non-allegorical interpretation is to be preferred here, particularly as nuts fit the ancient environment well. Ringgren suggests that the nut garden may be a symbolic reference to the underworld as a divine hiding-place: there was a valley in Lebanon dedicated to Artemis which was full of walnut trees. Pope (pp. 574–9) should be consulted for a full discussion of the significance of nuts: he traces many Ugaritic parallels and sketches their erotic associations. While discussing persistent belief in the quasi magical properties of nuts, he remarks strangely: "as one may observe in the window displays on the shelves of present-day 'organic' food shops"! These parallels quite clearly show that nuts were part of the natural scene around Lebanon: we have no need to allegorize. The erotic connexions are plain, particularly when we realize that **pomegranates** (following closely in this verse) were used as aphrodisiacs in Egypt.

12. Someone once called this the most difficult and obscure verse in the Song of Songs. It seems that the ancients found it difficult too, as their translations of it vary widely. A literal translation of the Heb. runs like this: "I did not know (*lô yāḏa'tî*)" – at which point comes the appropriate accent for marking the main division in the verse – "my soul set me (*năpšî sāmăṯnî*) chariots (*markᵉḇōṯ*) my willing people (*'ammî nāḏîḇ*)" – where neither "chariots" nor "my willing people" have any construction to fit into! LXX translates, "My soul did not know: the chariots of Aminadab placed me . . ." Vulg. corrects the position of the half-line pause in order to attempt better sense: "I did not know: my soul confused me because of Aminadab's chariots." Vulg.'s translation does at least construe and make sense – but who on earth is "Aminadab", and why should his chariots be famous? Vulg. is obviously trying to make sense of a text very close to the present MT (a case of Jerome correcting the LXX); but "confused" does not translate *sāmăṯnî* ("it/she placed me"), and no such preposition as "because of" exists in the Heb. The other Greek translators seem not to have seen in "Aminadab" a proper name as they largely reflect the same consonants as the Heb. but form them into different words: Aquila has "willing people" (*'am nāḏîḇ*; *nāḏîḇ* means "generous", a translation shared by Pesh.); Symmachus has "a leading people", again reflecting *nāḏîḇ* in a slightly different sense. Both appear to be correcting LXX's "Aminadab" according to a text remarkably like the present MT in the latter part of the verse.

Mention of chariots and a princely nobleman together with the numerous links discovered between the Song and Egyptian lyric poetry reminded Gerleman of prince Mehi, a character brought to scholarly attention by P. Smither in the *Journal of Egyptian Archaeology* 34 (1968), p. 116. In some Egyptian love lyrics Mehi plays a certain teasing role in the life of lovers which Smither himself likened to that of "a kind of Don Juan". This prince Mehi is further notable for driving chariots around, accompanied by an escort of young men. Gerleman suggests that in the Heb. Song Aminadab with his chariots may play the same sort of teasing tricks on the girl as Mehi does in the Egyptian songs. But the suggestion that Aminadab is the Heb. equivalent of the Egyptian Mehi rests on no solid ground: there is no evidence of such a figure in Heb. lore. In spite of the presumed loss of so much Heb. and Egyptian love poetry, Gerleman's suggestion is too fanciful. (For further information on prince Mehi see A. Hermann, *Altägyptische Liebesdichtung* (1959), pp. 105–8.)

G. R. Driver (*Festschrift für Alfred Bertholet* (1950), p. 136) abolishes the chariots by reading *mĕribbōṯ* for *markᵉḇōṯ* (not unreasonably, as the Heb. letters *b* and *k* are very alike): his suggestion underlies *NEB*'s rendering: "I did not know myself: she made me feel more than a prince reigning over myriads of people."

Fox (*VT* 33 (1985), pp. 206f.) suggested a translation very similar to that of *RSV*: "I do not know myself – you have put me in a chariot with a nobleman." He compares an Egyptian song in which a youth loses control of his body in lovesickness (it is, of course, not unknown for lovesickness to set people all of a dither!). The girl in the Song went to meet her lover in great excitement, i.e. ("before" she "was aware" of what was happening). It was as if she, a simple peasant girl, was placed in a chariot with a prince! Fox's suggestion requires a change of vocalization from *sāmăṯnî* (**my fancy set me**) to *sămtānî* ("you have put me") and the omission of one small consonant (a *yodh*) from *'ămmî*, "my people", to make *'īm*, "with" – but these are small problems compared with the mysterious, unknown Aminadab. Fox's suggestion may well be right, particularly in view of the fact that the royal fiction is often employed in these poems.

13. This verse is numbered differently in MT and *RSV*: in MT it starts the next chapter as 7:1 (thus all remaining verses in chapter 7 are numbered one higher in the Heb. text); but in *RSV* it is the last verse of chapter 6. It is another difficult, obscure verse: who is the **Shulammite**, and what is the **dance between two armies**? The problems start with the imperative **Return**. Vulg. and Pesh. both have this translation, reflecting MT *šûḇî* and presumably interpreting it of the girl being wooed by her lover back into the garden, the place of love. LXX, however, has "turn around, whirl", which fits the dancing motif well and involves reading the Heb. as *sōbbî*. The differences in the Heb. consonantal text are small. Although *sōbbî* is usually spelt with a *samech*, *samech* is occasionally written as a *sīn*; this differs from the stronger *šīn* only by a dot placed on the opposite end of the character – a dot that wouldn't appear in the original unvocalized text, anyway. So, if *sōḇbî* were spelt in that unusual way with a *sīn*, the two different forms would be identical in the unvocalized text, and the mistake could easily arise. *GNB* thus translates "dance", following LXX. *AB*, however, translates "leap", taking the verb as cognate with the Arabic *wa*ṯ*aba*, but Pope presents no evidence that this meaning for the verb was known in biblical Heb., or that "leap" should be preferred to "dance".

The second part of the verse is taken by some to come from a different speaker. If the verb **return** is meant to bring her back to enable people to **look upon the Shulammite** girl, then it seems natural that those people are addressed in the second part of the verse. Fox suggests that the girls of Jerusalem speak the first part of the verse and that the young men question them in the second part.

Various identifications of the **Shulammite** have been suggested; they have been listed by H. H. Rowley (*AJSL* 56 (1935), pp. 84–91) and, more briefly, by Fox (p. 157). In the Vaticanus tradition of the LXX she appears as *Sounamitis*, "girl of Shunem". This recalls Abishag the Shunammite, who was brought to king David in his old age to keep him warm (1 Kg. 1:1–3); later she was used by Solomon's mother as a pawn in the game of royal succession (1 Kg. 2:13–25). Whether Abishag actually entered Solomon's harem, as Goulder claims, is uncertain – if she did, it would explain well her mention here. But 1 Kg. mentions her only as a possible way for Adonijah to obtain the royal succession, and this is out of place here except in so far as her name may have become a cliché for feminine beauty (Gerleman). Albright ("Archaic Survivals in Canticles", *Hebrew and Semitic Studies presented to G. R. Driver*, p. 5) considers the name refers to the Mesopotamian war-goddess, Shulmānîtu, whose dance was said to be bloody battle. This would at least fit the **dance before two armies**. Suggestions that this is a sword-dance seem irrelevant. If "**dance**" (*sōbbî*) were preferred to return (*šûḇî*), then a case could be made for some sort of dance, though there is no mention of a sword: **return** makes acceptable sense in the first half of this verse, as argued above, and the terms used in the description in 7:1–6 do not demand, or even suggest, dancing.

As Goulder rightly observes, the use of *măh* (lit. "What?") in **Why should you look upon . . . ?** amounts to a negative (cf. *G-K* § 137bN). The final part of this verse runs literally: "(Why look upon the Shulammite) as upon the dances of two (military) camps/armies?" The dual, *măḥănăim*, has been thought by some to represent two parallel lines of dancers; but this is fanciful, particularly as none of the ancient versions translate "two" by either dual case or numeral "two". *măḥănăîm* need not be dual, as the consonantal spelling is identical with *meḥānîm*, the regular plural form found in Num. 13:19. That form was probably the original here, and it was altered later to fit the place-name, Maḥanaim, where Jacob met angels (Gen. 32:3) – a location well known to the historical books.

But, however these details may be expounded, this verse performs the function of bringing the girl back, as it were, from the nut garden or the nobleman's chariot, ready for the admiration expressed in the *waṣf* which follows in 7:1. As noted above, the editing hereabouts is less than skilful, and the seams are rather untidy.

RENEWED ADMIRATION OF THE BELOVED
7:1–5

This section contains the third *waṣf* of the Song, a second poem in praise of the girl. Modern commentators disagree about where the different songs should be divided here: such lack of clarity explains the confusion over chapter divisions noted above. The change of persons between 6:13 and 7:1 seems to indicate a change of poem: in 6:13 the second person plural, **you**, refers to the people admiring the Shulammite, whereas in 7:1 **your** is in the singular and is used of the **queenly maiden**. It thus becomes clear that the editorial function of the second half of 6:13 is to link the two poems together – this is Janus-type parallelism, as in 2:12. As in the other two *waṣfs* in 4:1–7 and 5:10–16, here the various bodily parts are described in an orderly sequence; but, whereas in the other two poems the order followed is downwards from top to toe, here the poem starts with the feet and moves upwards to the head. Some suggest this poem may have been placed here because of catchwords used: in the Heb. *băṯ nāḏîḇ*, **queenly maiden**, in 7:1 may pick up the phrase, *'ammî nāḏîḇ*, **beside my prince**, in 6:12; but see the notes above. In view of the fragmented continuity of the text in 6:11–13 this seems unlikely, and it is preferable to see the phrase, **Why should you look upon the Shulammite . . . ?** as an editorial link introducing quite naturally the praise of the girl's beauty that follows in 7:1–5.

7:1. The Heb. word used here for **feet** is unusual: the usual *răglăyĭm* is rejected for *paᵃmăyĭm*, used literally of feet only four times in the Bible. The word is used on another 114 occasions; its meanings include "hoof-beat", "step" and "blow", the most frequent being "stroke, occasion", whence the dual *paᵃmăyĭm*, "twice", especially in modern Heb. This usage of the word to mean "feet", infrequent in extant texts, may have been more common in lyric poetry which is now lost to us. **sandals** left the top of the foot almost completely bare, and for that reason were considered particularly alluring; cf. Jdt. 16:9, where it is said of Judith, after she had dressed herself deliberately to seduce Holofernes, that "her sandal ravished his eyes".

băṯ nāḏîḇ, here translated **queenly maiden**, means literally "daughter of a princely person" or "daughter of a prince"; *nāḏîḇ* means "noble, princely" in a general sense, with no suggestion of actual royalty. Vulg. took *băṯ nāḏîḇ* literally as "daughter of a leader", whereas LXX detected a proper name, "Nadab", which Aquila enthusiastically identified as Aminadab (cf. on 6:2 above). H. H. Hirschberg (*VT* 11 (1961), p. 378) suggested that *nāḏîḇ* was linked etymologically with the Arabic *nadb*, "fair, pretty". Heb. often uses *bēn*, "son", and *băṯ*, "daughter", in the construct with attributive words following to describe a particular condition or quality, cf. *kŏl-bĕn-ḥăyĭl* (1 Sam. 14:52), lit. "any son of power", *RSV* "any valiant man", and *bᵉnēy ʿōnî* (Prov. 31:5), lit. "sons of affliction". The word *nāḏîḇ* thus has nothing to do with actual royalty. **queenly** need not mean that, but use of that word in the English translation could be held to suggest a resumption of the royal travesty, which is by no means implied in the Heb. A better, more adequate translation would be "noble maiden".

Your rounded thighs takes the Heb. *ḥămmûqēy* as referring to the curves of the girl's legs. The Heb. word occurs only here, and some take it as referring to the whirling movements of the girl's dance. LXX's *rhythmoi* encourages this interpretation; but the Greek word means not only "rhythm" or "measured action" but

also the "form" or "shape" of a thing. So the LXX translation here cannot be used to support views that a dance is necessarily described. But **jewels** seem strange objects of comparison with **thighs**, even if **rounded**. Ancient translators toiled over this: Symmachus translated "the joints of your thighs are like (as delicate as?) necklaces" – so too Vulg. Fox suggests either "the place where your thigh turns" (with Ibn Ezra) or "your (curved) buttocks". Perhaps we should accept that well-rounded thighs rather than slim legs were admired in the ancient world.

The Heb. word for **a master hand** has been shown by M. Ellenbogen (*Foreign Words in the Old Testament* (1962), p. 30) to be a loan-word from the Accadian *ummānu* and the Sumerian *umman*, both "artisan, craftsman". This word is greeted by Gerleman with considerable enthusiasm as support for his view that the poet is using architectural terms of statuary to describe the girl. But Gerleman is not necessarily right: we today may compliment a girl on her complexion, saying it is "without blemish" or "pure as a statue" or even "statuesque", so what prevents an ancient poet from suggesting the same comparison? Parts of the description in this passage may compare the girl to a perfect statue, but that does not mean that the whole of the description needs to be understood in such a way.

2. If the order of bodily parts, from bottom to top, is followed consistently, the **navel** is in the wrong position between thighs and belly: it comes above those. The part of the girl's body mentioned here is therefore more likely to be the vagina or vulva than the navel (so Goulder). The Heb. word *šŏrrēḵ*, **Your navel**, is philologically equivalent to the Arabic *surratu*, "navel", though Rudolph suggests that comparison with the Arabic *sirr* is more apt: this word is used for the private, sexual parts of a woman's body, possibly "vulva" here. The Heb. word used here for **bowl**, *'ăggān*, is used of a bowl for offerings in Exod. 24:6 and of bowl-shaped flagons in Isa. 22:24. Fox cites large, two-handled, ring-based bowls from Palmyra and Petra with "AGGAN" inscribed on them. Gerleman claims that in Egyptian pictorial art and sculpture the navel is conventionally portrayed with stark clarity as a wide, round hole. Here Gerleman's continual reference to things Egyptian certainly makes good sense, and seems to explain satisfactorily why the **navel** should be compared to **a rounded bowl**. His suggestion is superior to J. Reider's view (*HUCA* 2 (1928), p. 4) that, on the basis of the Arabic *gawnatu*, "disc of the moon", the Heb. *'ăggān* here expresses the concavity of the navel, the mixture of light and dark being caused by the relief on the bowl. L. Kopf (*VT* 6 (1956), p. 293) claimed that Reider had misused the Arabic dictionaries and that the Arabic word referred primarily to colour, not shape.

But it seems unlikely that the lover would say of the navel that it **never lacks mixed wine**. These words could have been added as further description of the bowl, just as **the work of a master hand** describes the **jewels** in v. 1 and **twins of a gazelle** describes the **fawns** in v. 3. But what is the point of stating that some **wine** is left in the cup? How does this add to the description? An explicitly sexual interpretation makes better sense, with the **mixed wine** referring delicately to the mingling of the male and female bodily secretions at the appropriate place on the girl's body.

To liken a lady's **belly** to **a heap of wheat** seems to us similarly indecorous. Is the point of the comparison the round shape of such a heap or its colour, probably yellow? Possibly a blend of both: a gently curved belly with a tawny hue. Piles of wheat were sometimes **encircled** by a thorn hedge to prevent scattering in a wind or casual grazing by animals. But for a precious **heap** like the Shulammite's belly, a hedge of **lilies** is more decorous and appropriate. Neither **heap** nor **lilies** should be taken too literally – they are only stylistic, part of the lyric description.

3. This verse is identical with 4:5 (see notes there), except that here are omitted the words, **that feed among the lilies**, used of the gazelle's fawns. In the last two chapters of the book there is a good deal of repetition of sentiments already expressed: the poetry is very uneven in quality.

4. The beloved's **neck** is compared to **an ivory tower**. This recalls the similar comparison in 4:4, where her neck was likened to **the tower of David, built for an arsenal**; however, this time there are no shields (multiple necklaces) hanging round the tower. The colour, **ivory**, implies a refined, pale complexion in an often humid climate, but also creates an air of luxury, as panels of ivory were much used in expensive buildings like palaces at Samaria (1 Kg. 22:39) and elsewhere (Amos 3:15; Ps. 45:8). Comparison of the human complexion to ivory was a well-known compliment in the ancient world, and is found in Homer. The length of the girl's **neck** need not worry us: in Fox's Egyptian song no. 31 the boy says admiringly of his beloved that she is "long of neck" – long necks were clearly admired.

Your eyes are pools in Heshbon: *RSV*'s translation follows the Heb. exactly. The two other comparisons in this verse (**neck** and **nose**) both have **like** translating the Heb. particle *k*ᵉ. This particle is strangely absent with the **eyes**, although LXX, Pesh. and Vulg. all supply "like" here too; so perhaps the *kaph* has been omitted here in error by haplography, as the previous Heb. word, *'ēynăyik̲*, ends with a *kaph*. Also, **in Heshbon** (*b*ᵉ*ḥesbōn*) begins with a *beth*, so, as *beth* and *kaph* are easily confused in shape, this similarity could have led scribes to omit the *beth* before **pools** (*b*ᵉ*rēk̲ōt̲*), which follows immediately on **Your eyes** with its final *kaph*. Aquila translates **Heshbon** as "in reflexion", as from the root *ḥšb*. Some early Christian exegetes did likewise, but in view of the place-names that follow (**Lebanon**, **Damascus**, **Carmel**) it is likely that the well-known Moabite town in Transjordan is intended.

RSV is probably correct in translating *ša'ar bat̲-rabbîm* as **the gate of Bath-rabbim**, i.e. the gate leading to Bath Rabbim (lit. "daughter of many" – the word "daughter" is often used of villages crowding round a city). City gates were often called by the town or village they led towards (cf. the Damascus and Jaffa gates in Jerusalem even today). That a place (or gate) called Bath Rabbim in Heshbon is unknown does not make this view impossible; we don't know the topography well, and the Targumic rendering, "house of many", reflecting *bēyt̲ rabbîm* in Heb., may well indicate change to a name known to the Targumist. G. S. Glanzman (*CBQ* 23 (1961), p. 229, n. 11) suggested that it was a well-known place-name which we happen not to know now, and he may well be right. As no symbolic meaning is obvious, it is likely that the name refers to a real gate at Heshbon.

Your nose is like a tower of Lebanon: long necks may have been admired, but enormous noses were not, as Goulder observes.

Unless the **tower of Lebanon** was a specific locality unknown to us, the parallel is probably with the eastern side of the anti-Lebanon ridge, which falls away steeply down to Damascus.

5. The upward progression of the description concludes with the **head**. But is it complimentary to compare a lady's head with **Carmel**? Mount Carmel is the high mountain ridge running for over ten miles between the Jezreel valley and the Mediterranean coast: its highest point reaches c. 1,240 feet. It lies between the plain and the sea at an oblique angle to the coastline, projecting onto the coast at Haifa, where it forms a particularly prominent headland. Carmel is mentioned elsewhere as a notable mountain: its majesty is celebrated in Isa. 35:27; Amos' words that the top of Carmel withers when the Lord roars from Zion (1:2) testify to its fertility; and in Jer. 46:18 "Carmel by the sea" is likened to the isolated Mount Tabor. The term is no insult to a handsome head. But a similar word (*karmîl* – its second vowel is different but it is otherwise identical) means "purple" in 2 Chr. 2:7, 14; 3:14. The use of *kᵉ'argāman*, **like purple**, later in this verse suggests that Fox correctly detects here another Janus pun (cf. on 2:12): **Carmel** refers to the mountain ridge as **Heshbon**, **Lebanon** and **Damascus** refer to real places in v. 4, but it also looks forward to her **flowing locks . . . like purple**. Goulder, without good cause, tries to relieve the possible embarrassment of likening a girl's head to a mountain by glossing the translation with the words, "(Carmel) with the forests on its brow": but those words are not present in the Heb. – wordplay is auditory, not visual.

your flowing locks recalls the comparison of the girl's hair to **a flock of goats, moving down** mountain slopes in 4:1; she evidently has a tumbling hairstyle of the sort which is well attested in Egyptian art. But why is her hair described as being **like purple**? Either her hair was purple or it wasn't! The Heb. *kaph* probably has its asseverative use here: "truly purple". But, as G. R. Driver remarked, doesn't purple hair seem somewhat peculiar? According to Pliny, Tyrian purple was a particularly rich, glossy colour. Gerleman cites a special technique used by Egyptian workers in bronze whereby streaks of gold (or purple?) were inlaid on statues. In Greek lyric poetry "purple" often denoted rich, dark hair colour. Another possibility is that the accent under *'argāmān*, "purple", divides the verse wrongly: *'argāmān* should perhaps be construed in the construct before *mělěḵ*, "king", to mean "royal purple": this would bring the description to a suitable climax before its close. The word *dallōṯ* in the phrase, *dallōṯ rō'šěḵ*, **your flowing locks**, is used elsewhere only in Isa. 38:12 of a weaver's loom: thus the poet may here be using technical weaving terms to describe the richness of the maiden's hair. Gerleman also detected such technical terms behind the **tresses** (*rᵉhāṭîm*) at the end of the verse: the Heb. word is used elsewhere (Gen. 30:38, 41; Ex. 2:16) of water troughs or conduits for cattle to drink from. The same root underlies *rahîṭēnū* in 1:17 above, where the word may denote long beams. Gerleman suggests that *rᵉhāṭîm* may here be used of the beams that held the frame of the weaver's loom, the hair being compared to the handsome material stretched between them.

How, then, is the **king . . . held captive in the tresses**? Any psychological image seems wrong in this objective description: he is not bewitched by her hair. Nor does any analogy with the judge Samson help. *NEB* revocalizes *mělěḵ*, "king", as *millēḵ*, "your hair", and translates, "your tresses (are braided with ribbons)". Such a rare word could easily have been overlaid by the royal fiction so prominent in these poems. But the idea of a young man ("king") being captivated by beautiful hair is not as modern as some might suppose: in Fox's Egyptian poem no. 43 the boy says, "With her hair she lassoes me", and, if Fox's reconstruction of no. 3 is correct, the boy claims his beloved's "hair is the bait in the trap to ensnare" him. Fox translates our passage, "a king is captured by the locks", having taken the previous phrase technically of weaving: "the thrums of your head are like purple". Thus the *waṣf* comes to its climax with the mention of the king and royal purple, the royal fiction forming a suitable conclusion.

A FRAGMENTARY POEM OF ADMIRATION
7:6–9

Following the reasonably complete *waṣf* in 7:1–5 comes a much shorter song which admires the girl in a similarly descriptive style but with a different emphasis. Instead of following an orderly description of bodily parts, this poem starts in v. 6 with an exclamation of the girl's beauty, which then leads to a general description of her stature and her breasts in v. 7, using the image of a palm tree. In v. 8 the image is extended to illustrate the young man's passionate wish to claim his girl, i.e. he climbs up the tree. The poem closes in v. 9 with an erotic description of kissing. Closely linked to this poem are the four verses which follow (vv. 10–13); here, after the sensuousness of vv. 8–9, the lovers go off together – another example of the editor's skilful placing of the poems.

6. The rhetorical question at the beginning of this verse is rightly interpreted by *RSV* as an exclamation. The second part of the verse has caused difficulty: literally the Heb. means "love in delights" (*'ahᵃḇāh battaᵃnūgîm*). Whether abstract is used for concrete and the noun "love" is used to denote the person, the object of love (as in common speech today) is uncertain. Such a usage is recognized by Vulg. (*carissima*) and *RSV* (**O loved one**), but *NEB* preferred to change the noun to a passive participle, *ᵃhûḇāh*. *RSV*'s **delectable maiden**, like *NEB*'s "daughter of delights", follows Pesh. and reads *baṯ taᵃnūgîm*, assuming haplography of the *t*. The evidence for this reading is very early, as even Aquila, correcting LXX by the Heb. text of his day, has "daughter of delights". *RSV* has smoothed out this literal rendering into good English.

7. The first half of this verse seems to contain another Janus pun (see on 2:12). *RSV* margin ("This your stature is") draws attention to the unusual Heb. construction here: demonstrative adjectives normally have the definite article along with the noun they qualify (cf. *laḥmēnū hazzeh*, "this our bread" or "this bread of ours"), unless they form the predicate of a nominal sentence (cf. *zeh laḥmēnū*, Jos. 9:12, "here is our bread" (lit. "this is our bread") and *zeh hayyām*, Ps. 104:25, "yonder is the sea" (lit. "this is the sea")). So here in *zō'ṯ qōmāṯēḵ dāmᵉṯāh*, **you are stately** (lit. "this – your stature – is like . . .") – where "your stature" (*qōmāṯēḵ*) both completes the nominal sentence, "this is your stature", and provides the subject for the verb *dāmᵉṯāh*, "your stature is like . . ." – the word *qōmāṯēḵ*, points both ways. This construction has no parallel in English, and *RSV* rightly paraphrases it. However, **stately** is hardly the best word to describe stature – though the picture of a long, narrow palm tree adequately suggests that the girl is standing straight. The primary point of the comparison is the girl's slimness – with the fruits of enjoyment thrown in. It is unnecessary for Goulder to suggest that the comparison only makes sense if her arms are waved aloft like palm branches, with her breasts "like the clusters of dates growing on the stem where the fronds begin" – surely this is a strange position for breasts.

The Heb. word *'aškōlōṯ* (**its clusters**) was usually used of grape clusters, though usage was clearly wider, as shown by 1:14, where the word is used of henna blossoms. Grapes do not grow on palm trees, so date panicles must be intended here. According to ancient writers various sorts of dates differed considerably in colour, shape and size: dates could even be globular like apples. Female breasts seem to us today not at all like clusters of dates: we admire supported, well-shaped breasts. But in those countries where women go about naked to the waist female breasts are seen in their natural condition – unsupported and in their shape not unlike clusters of dates hanging down. This is realistic imagery at the rustic level rather than royal travesty. Such rustic imagery is then continued in order to express the girl's inaccessibility: to win her requires considerable effort, like that needed to climb a palm tree and pick its dates (as in v. 8).

8. I say: this remark seems superfluous, stating the self-evident. The verb *'āmartî* is here used probably in its looser sense of thought or intention, and Goulder's "I thought" or even *AB*'s "methinks" suit the meaning well. The Heb. verb is in the perfect tense but has a present meaning, as often with verbs describing cerebral processes.

To **climb the palm tree and lay hold of its branches** has been thought to imply vigorous sexual activity. Goulder certainly thought so, and believed that the passage referred to the young man climbing on his beloved and delighting in her breasts. But climbing a palm tree is very different from tumbling in an embrace. In any case, sexual pleasure is usually symbolized in the Song by sweetness of taste or smell rather than by actions: it is more likely that the climbing here is secondary to obtaining the fruit, without any specific sexual activity implied. Palm branches sprout quite a long way up the tree, and the only way to harvest the dates is to climb the tree, which involves considerable effort: in *Nat. Hist.* 13:26 Pliny gives a graphic description of people climbing to the very tops of palm trees to gather dates.

The Heb. word used here, *sansinnāyw*, **its branches**, is clearly related to the Accadian *sinsinnu*, "date panicle". Fox suggests that the Heb. refers either to the maiden's arms or to her hair: in 5:11 the man's locks were compared to *taltallîm*, probably palm fronds. In a general metaphor it is unnecessary to treat every word in an exact way: someone climbing a date palm would naturally grasp its main branches for support; he would hardly grasp the panicles of fruit. The comparison with the Accadian word should not be pressed too far: the Heb. word may refer generally to the green growth on the tree – in 5:11 to leafy fronds, here to the branches. Certainly **breasts** are not like **clusters of the vine** in knobby detail: the likeness is rather to the grapes' sweet taste. The comparisons here are sensual, but not visual.

In the last part of the verse the imagery continues to be sensual, but this time the sense of smell is evoked: **the scent of your breath** is **like apples**. This probably refers to the nose kiss, a gesture of affection which is claimed to have been frequent in the ancient East: the couple would rub their faces together and smell each other's noses. The custom is illustrated by Fox's Egyptian poem no. 12, where the girl says to the boy, "The scent of your nose alone is what revives my heart."

9. In the first part of this verse the young man continues his *waṣf*. **your kisses** translates *ḥiqqēk*, lit. "your palate". The same word was used in the *waṣf* in 5:16, where *RSV* translated, "his speech"; but we found a literal translation preferable, to make the verse fit the physical character of the *waṣf*. But more than a strictly visual comparison is implied here by **like the best wine**: lips don't *look* like good wine – rather, they *feel* like it when they are kissed. This sensual meaning probably applies in 5:16 also. *RSV* correctly translates *yēyn haṭṭōḇ* as **the best wine**. Heb. has no comparative or superlative forms of adjectives: writers had to use adjectives defined by the article, e.g. *the good one* = the best (cf. *G-K* §§126x, 133h). *ṭōḇ* could also refer to a particular type of wine, as *qāneh haṭṭōḇ* in Jer. 6:20 means a type of "sweet cane" or *calamus aromaticus*. The cognate Arabic *ṭayyaba*, "embalmed", shares the same root.

The feminine possessive suffix in **your kisses** (*ḥiqqēḵ*) shows that the lover's *waṣf* continues. But after the first three words a problem arises: **that goes down** translates the masculine participle *hōlēḵ*, clearly agreeing with **the best wine**. In the Heb. there follows *lᵉḏōḏi* ("for my lover" in *RSV* margin). But *dōḏ* in this sense is never used of the girl by the man – always of the man by the girl; here the man seems to use it of the girl – contrary to usage elsewhere. So *RSV* omits the word from its text, giving a translation of it in the margin with no further comment. But all the ancient translations show knowledge of the word and provide for a change of speaker. Such a change irrupts very suddenly into the half-completed *waṣf*. According to Fox, the girl becomes impatient, interrupts her lover and completes the sentence, "reciprocating his desire". Fox even suggests that "his desire and hers are in such harmony that they can be uttered in a single sentence". This is taking things too far, as there is no other example of such sudden interruption, and elsewhere the lovers' dialogue is remarkably formal. Gerleman thinks the girl's reply spreads syntactically into the next verse, **the best wine** acting as predicate to the subject **I** in v. 10: "a wine, flowing . . . and dripping . . . am I for my beloved". This is ingenious, but the construction is complicated and, in order to be really intelligible, would need "wine" to be repeated. However, the plural *dōḏîm* means love as an abstract quality, or even love-making (cf. Prov. 7:18). *NEB*, retaining the consonants of *lᵉḏōḏî*, reads the plural, *lᵉḏōḏăy*, "(to welcome) my caresses", which may be right. *lᵉmēyšārîm*, **smoothly**, recalls *bᵉmēyšārîm*, used of swallowed wine in Prov. 23:31. It is unnecessary to detect here with Goulder a hint of male sexual "uprightness" (i.e. erection) from the usual sense of the adjective *yāšār*, "straight, upright".

A literal translation of the final three words of the verse (*dôḇēḇ sip̄ṯēy yᵉšēnîm*) seems to be, "dripping through the lips of sleepers": but, as G. R. Driver pointed out (with characteristic vigour) in his lectures, that would be fatal, as the sleepers would choke.

The ancient translations reflect **(lips) and teeth** (*w*[e]*šinnîm*) for "of sleepers" (*y*[e]*šēnîm*), a reading which in the consonantal text involves the very easy confusion of a short vertical stroke (*y*) with a full length one (*w*) – a simple correction which counters Driver's objection and makes good sense.

A COUNTRY WALK FOR LOVERS
7:10–13

After the *waṣf* addressed to the girl by her lover in 7:6–9, there comes a summons from the girl to her lover: she wishes him to accompany her on a short walk in the country – a common enough theme for lovers in all ages. Love in gardens is a theme frequently found in Egyptian love lyrics (cf. Fox, pp. 283–5). Here, as in 2:10–14, the lovers seem to aim for open country rather than any particular garden. The imagery of fruit, frequently met in love lyrics, builds up to pomegranates (v. 12) and especially to mandrakes (v. 13), which the girl has **laid up** for her lover (mandrakes are well known for their aphrodisiac qualities). So, even though this poem is short and similar to passages elsewhere, it certainly has a climax in its own right.

10. I am my beloved's and his desire is for me: words that echo the formula of mutual possession already found in 2:16 and 6:3. But there is a very significant difference: the second half of the formula, **and my beloved is mine**, here becomes **and his desire is for me**. So the possession is no longer mutual: the girl appears to be dominant here. This is particularly notable when we realize that the Heb. word for **his desire** (*t*[e]*šûqāṯô*) is used elsewhere in the OT only in Gen. 3:16: *w*[e]*'ĕl 'îšēḵ t*[e]*šûḵāṯēḵ w*[e]*hû' yimšol-bāḵ* – "yet your desire shall be for your husband, and he shall rule over you". If we had greater knowledge of vocabulary usage outside the Bible, this might not be significant, as we might encounter much wider use of *t*[e]*šûqāh*. But, as it is, here in the Song we seem to have an echo of Gen. 3:16 in reverse: whereas there the woman's husband is to rule over her, here the man's passion for the woman is such that she controls him – a radically different situation! As Gordis notes, the woman's subservience to the man becomes very different here, where the poet expresses the lovers' joyous desire for each other; perhaps her desirability gives her the upper hand. This variation seems to change the whole balance between the sexes.

11. The theme of 2:10 reappears in vv. 11 and 12; but there the lover entices his girl away into the open country, whereas here it is she who summons him. In both poems spring-like weather is important as the setting for love scenes, as are strolls and country walks: such themes are found in the Egyptian love songs without any connotation of sacred marriage. Indeed, country walks are not unknown for lovers today!

After going **forth into the fields** the couple are to **lodge in the villages** (*bakkᵉp̄ārîm*). **lodge** is a good translation for *nālînāh*, which means simply "lodge for the night", without any suggestion of sexual activity, which some may detect behind *NEB*'s "to lie down among the henna bushes" or even Fox's "spend the night in the countryside". *bakkᵉp̄ārîm* can be taken two ways: *RSV*, with LXX and Vulg., speaks of lodging **in the villages**, whereas *NEB* has "among the henna bushes". *kōp̄ĕr* has two distinct meanings: an unwalled village, and henna bushes or flowers and cosmetics from that plant (cf. 1:4 and 4:13). Fox claims to find another Janus pun here, as in 2:13 and 7:6: the same word looks both backwards to **villages** in the countryside amid fields, and forwards to the plants and flowers of v. 12. There may be such a double reference here, but it is not as notable as the other instances are. Goulder prefers to translate "in the henna" here because "an ancient village hostel is likely to have been dirty and sordid" – but here he is mistakenly applying modern standards of hygiene. Ringgren's emendation of *bakkᵉp̄ārîm* to *bakkᵉrāmîm*, "in the vineyards", to fit the next verse, has no versional support and seems unjustified.

12. It is uncertain how far the invitation to **go out early to the vineyards** lies in direct sequence to the lodging **in the villages** of v. 11. The use of fruit images for sexual enjoyment in the Song might suggest that a rosy glow adorns the world of nature after a night of love. Many of the fruits specified here were mentioned in 4:13–15, where the garden appeared to be the girl herself – this was made plain by 4:16, where the young man was invited to **come to his garden, and eat its choicest fruits**, and by 5:1, where he triumphantly entered it. But this takes it all too literally: if such a close temporal sequence were intended, the lover's promise at the end of the verse, **There I will give you my love**, comes far too late in the programme of events – after a night of lovemaking!

pittăḥ, **(the grape blossoms) have opened**, is a Piel form which is usually transitive and intensive. But here any transitive force is lost in an unusual intransitive use – unless we assume ellipse of the object ("buds" or the like). Gerleman and Rudolph both suggested reading the Niphal, *nip̄tăḥ*, the initial *nun* being lost by haplography following the previous word, *haggĕp̄ĕn*. But the intensive form of this root is used intransitively in the Arabic *fattaḥa*, "opened up" of buds, and a similarly intransitive use of this verb appears in Isa. 48:18, *lō' pittᵉḥāh 'ŏznᵉḵā*, "your ear has not opened": so there is no need to emend the text here. On the meaning of *sᵉmāḏar*, **grape blossoms**, see the note on 2:13. As in 1:2, 4 and 4:10, LXX and Vulg. insist on vocalizing *dōḏay*, **my love**, as *dădday*, "my breasts" – the two words are indistinguishable in unvocalized script. We should note the assonance between *dōḏay* and *haddûḏā'îm*, **The mandrakes**, the first word in the next verse.

13. It seems quite likely that the Heb. word translated **mandrakes**, *dûḏā'îm*, is related to *dōḏay*, "my beloved" (if not also to *daddîm*, "breasts"). Identification of the plant to which the Heb. refers with the mandragora, or mandrake, is technically uncertain, as the Heb. word may be used as a collective term for plants with narcotic or aphrodisiac qualities; but this identification was certainly known by the time of the LXX translation of this passage. Outside the Song, mandrakes occur in the Bible only in Gen. 30:14–16, where Reuben brings some to his mother, Leah, to promote her fertility. They occur several times in the Egyptian love songs: in Fox's poem no. 2 the girl says to the boy, "your love is mixed in my body . . . like mandragoras in which gum is mixed", and in no. 20B she says his love "is like a mandragora in a man's hand". The yellow-flowering mandragora, common in Southern Palestine and Egypt, was said to produce love-apples, a term probably referring to the tuberous growth of the roots, which were believed to have aphrodisiac qualities. The erotic overtones of this in love poetry are obvious.

Why should **all choice fruits** be placed **over our doors**? The plural, **doors**, need not worry us (it worried the *NEB* translators, who emended to the singular): generalizing plurals are not uncommon in poetry (cf. *G-K* § 124e). There is thus no need to ask how many doors Egyptian houses had. Goulder points out that doors are used in Talmudic Heb. as sexual euphemisms; but in this instance the meaning of the Song's text includes no such overtones – Talmudic Hebrew is much later. Fox preferred a less exact translation: "at our openings", including windows. As mandrakes give off their scent in the open countryside, the girl is probably talking about a "house" or booth in a rural setting like that in 1:16–17.

Rudolph seems uncertain about the significance of **new as well as old**. It is unnecessary to search for precise meaning in the imagery here: the Song does not lend itself to such exact (or allegorical) interpretation, any more than the Egyptian lyrics do (*pace* Targum, Jewish midrash and some Christian commentators). The phrase essentially means "of all kinds" – it is a way of describing totality. She has **laid up** for her lover the very best delights of love: here she repeats and further elaborates her promise at the end of v. 12 to give him her love.

BACK TO MOTHER'S HOUSE
8:1–4

Scholars have disagreed over where the break between the songs occurs here. Gerleman discerned a distinct break between 7:11–12, where the lovers' rendezvous lies in fields, villages and vineyards, and 7:13, a verse which by its reference to **doors** is linked more naturally to the girl's mother's house in 8:2. He therefore placed the break after 7:12, taking 7:13 with 8:1–4. But the **mandrakes** and **choice fruits** of 7:13 suggest a link with the **grape blossoms** and **pomegranates** of 7:12: all of these are exotic plants cited to enhance the heightening, climactic atmosphere in 7:13, where the girl is laying up erotic pleasures for her lover.

Surely all this eroticism is not the best introduction for the potential mother-in-law of 8:2. Further, in 8:1 comes a clear change of mood. No longer are flowers and fruit mentioned in abundance: the emphasis lies rather on the girl bringing her lover home to her mother's house. Again, the rendezvous in 8:1–4 is the girl's family home; she no longer tries to hide away in the fields with her lover, but now wants their relationship to be openly recognized. For all these reasons it seems justifiable to start a new section at 8:1.

The beloved seeks public acceptance, like the girl in Fox's Egyptian poem no. 36, whose mother seems on the verge of recognizing the couple's love. The girl there says:

If only mother knew my heart –
she would go inside for a while.
O Golden One, put that into her heart!
Then I could hurry to (my) brother
and kiss him before his company,
and not be ashamed because of anyone.

In neither the Heb. poem nor the Egyptian one is the lovers' meeting pictured in rustic fantasy: the girl wants their relationship to be out in the open – she even wishes she was his sister, so that kissing him in public might be respectable! We should note an additional likeness to the Egyptian poems: in both cultures the girl's mother plays some part, however small, in the lovers' experience.

8:1. Any theory that the Song consists of a cycle of wedding songs falls decisively at this point: a properly betrothed fiancée would hardly wish that her lover would behave **like a brother** to her! The love of these two for each other is still secret: she doesn't really wish he was her brother, although the preposition *k*ᵉ in *kʿāh* (**like a brother**), usually **like**, can also be asseverative; cf. *NEB*, "if only you were my own true brother!", which takes it too far. The point is simply that she wishes to be able to kiss him openly and unashamedly. Only common prostitutes kissed strange men in the street (cf. Prov. 7:12f.), but sisters could always kiss brothers. There is thus no need to detect mythical motifs either in the sisterly relationship or in nursing at one's

mother's breast: breast-feeding lasted for longer in a child's life then – sucking at breasts was even practised by adults, cf. Fox's Egyptian poem no. 1, where the girl says: "Take my breasts that their gift may flow to you."

The Heb. *'eššāqᵉḵā*, **I would kiss you**, may well be a deliberate play on words to suggest *'ašqᵉḵā*, "let me drench you (with kisses)", as with *yiššāqēnî* and *yaškēnî* in 1:2.

2. This short poem develops further as the girl's imagination leads her thoughts on: the wish and conditional clause of v. 1 now become a firm intention expressed by a straightforward future tense: she will lead her lover from where she met him, **outside** (v. 1), **into the house of** her **mother**. *RSV* then follows LXX and Pesh., reading **and into the chamber of her that conceived me**; these words certainly make an excellent poetic balance for **into the house of my mother** earlier in the verse, but they are not in the Heb. text here. The same wording in similar parallelism occurred in 3:4, where the girl was also portrayed as leading her lover to her mother's house. It is likely that LXX and Pesh. have here completed the phrase for themselves according to the usage of 3:4. But the MT here reads differently: for **and into the chamber of her that conceived me** it has *tᵉlammᵉdēnî*, "you/she [the two verbal forms are indistinguishable] will teach me", a reading supported by Vulg.'s *me docebis*. Jerome here, as elsewhere, seems to have corrected the LXX tradition according to the Heb. text before him. This agreement of Vulg. with MT shows that the LXX text is probably a corruption of an original *tᵉlammᵉḏēnî* into *tēlᵉḏēnî*, an omission in the original consonantal text of only one letter – *m*. The closeness of these words may well have led to the confusion with 3:4 noted above. Gordis thought that confusion arose for the LXX translators between *hôrᵉṯāh*, "she taught", and *hārᵉṯāh*, "she conceived", an error which led them to repeat the words from the earlier verse; but the tenses are quite wrong for this interpretation. The Vulg. reading shows MT to be original – but what does "you will teach me" really mean in this context? It sounds rather as if the girl expects the young man to show her what to do, or, more properly, leaves the initiative in love-making to him. That seems a suitable sense.

G. R. Driver claimed to have found another meaning for the

Heb. root *LMD* from usage in Syriac and Ethiopic. Payne Smith's dictionary gives the Syriac verb *'ettalmed* as "embraced", and the Ethiopic *lamada* could mean "be friendly, embrace". But Payne Smith gives as the object of "embrace" the monastic life! This hardly suits the natural, erotic interpretation of the Song.

The **spiced wine** may well suggest kissing: in 1:2 the girl's love was **better than wine**, in 7:9 her kisses were likened to **the best wine** and we interpreted the reference to the lover's **speech** in 5:16 as meaning his mouth, the kisses of which were **most sweet**. In **the juice of my pomegranates** *RSV* invents a plural ending to the Heb. noun, which reads the singular, "my pomegranate". This use of the possessive pronoun is thought to show that the girl is using "pomegranate" figuratively to mean her breast: here we probably have another reference to adult sucking of the breasts, as in v. 1.

3. We have already noted that many phrases in the last two chapters echo earlier passages. This verse can hardly be called an echo: it is rather an almost exact repetition of 2:6, with just one difference – here **under** translates *tăḥăṯ*, whereas in 2:6 *tăḥăṯ* is prefixed by the preposition *l^e*, whence *l^{e}ṯăḥăṯ*. But this makes no difference to the sense. The closeness of this link with 2:6 is shown by the fact that, although this verse is part of a poem in which the lover is addressed in the second person in vv. 1 and 2, in v. 3 he is spoken of in the third person, as in 2:6. This could be explained, one supposes, as the maiden making a hushed aside under her breath for the audience (though not her lover) to hear. But it would be wrong to press this change of person too far. One of the features of the Song is what Fox calls "associative sequences" (cf. pp. 215–17), whereby linked verses reappear together in similar contexts. Thus in vv. 3f. the girl expresses her wish for her lover's embrace, using the same words as she 2:6: in both passages this wish is followed by an adjuration addressed to the daughters of Jerusalem not to stir or awaken love (cf. 2:7, 8:4). Indeed, the same adjuration is used in 3:5 also, where it is preceded by a reference to the maiden's house similar to that in 8:2. This clear association with 2:6 probably led to the third person being used here, as in that passage – against the consistency of 8:1–3.

4. The "associative sequence" continues with a verse which is worded exactly like 2:7 and 3:5 except for two differences in the Heb. First, in the words, **that you stir not up nor awaken love**, this passage twice uses the unusual negative *mah* (cf. *G-K* § 137b) instead of *'im*, which is used in the other two passages. *'im* is the word usually used in Heb. oaths and, indeed, it is read by some Heb. MSS here. *mah* is properly an interrogative pronoun, "what . . . ?", or an exclamation, "how . . . !"; but it seems sometimes to have a negative force, like the Arabic *ma*: this rare meaning may have arisen from the use of this word in rhetorical questions (cf. *G-K* § 137b). Secondly, the abstract noun **love** may have been understood to mean the loved one (as often in northern English dialects) rather than the quality. Certainly Vulg. seems to have understood it this way, as it translates *dilectam*, "loved one" (fem.) – unless Jerome was translating accurately a Heb. text which read *ʼᵃhûḇāh*, passive participle, "the loved one", with the *u* not written out fully with consonantal *waw*. *NEB* took this latter interpretation by translating, "Do not disturb my love until she is ready", and claimed to read *ʼᵃhûḇāh*. The difference is not great but the sense is clearer.

A FRAGMENT – OR TWO?
8:5

In the rather badly ordered last chapter of the Song this verse seems isolated. The previous poem (vv. 1–4) described the lovers' rendezvous and the girl's subsequent passionate invitation of her lover into her mother's house. The poem then concluded with an adjuration to the daughters of Jerusalem, who had previously rounded poems off in this way in 2:7, 3:5 and 5:8. Verses 6 and 7 of this chapter contain a short poem describing the power of love. Verse 5 is thus separated off in both directions. Moreover, as shown in the commentary below, it is made up of several unrelated echoes of previous poems in the Song; so this verse is not only isolated from its neighbours – it is even fragmentary within itself.

5. The question, **Who is that coming up from the wilder-**

ness, leaning up on her beloved? refers to both male and female lovers in the third person. In vv. 1–3 the girl spoke in the first person of her lover in the third person; in the first part of this verse she is described in the third person as **leaning upon her beloved**, with her lover in the third person also. But this changes: in the second part of the verse she speaks in the first person of waking her lover, whom she addresses directly in the second person. Already the verse has fallen into two disparate sections: in the second part of it the girl is clearly addressing her lover, but the first part must be spoken by some third party, possibly the poet or the daughters of Jerusalem acting as a chorus.

Who is that coming up from the wilderness has in the Heb. exactly the same wording as the beginning of 3:6, a fact which *RSV* conceals by translating *mî zō'ṯ* in different ways: in 3:6 we read **What is that . . .**, here **Who is that . . .** These translations differ presumably because the answer to the question is different in each passage: in 3:6 it is the (inanimate and impersonal) **litter of Solomon**, here it is the girl on her beloved's arm. *RSV*, in order to make a good translation, uses two different interrogative pronouns, but unfortunately this hides the identical wording of the Heb. in both passages: the words in 8:5 have been taken unchanged from 3:6 – one of the "echoes" referred to above.

That this passage doesn't fit together well is further shown by the rest of the verse: is the young man asleep **Under the apple tree** or is he on a journey, **coming up from the wilderness**, supporting his beloved? He can't be doing both, which is what this verse seems to suggest. This is more evidence of fragmentary continuity of the text. Links with other verses seem to be lacking, although scholars have suggested that a link with the previous verse may lie in *'ôrărtîḵā*, **I awakened you**, which comes from the same root as *t^e'ôr^erû*, **awaken**, in v. 4.

the apple tree has inspired much theological symbolism of the kind discussed in the Afterword. In 2:3 the girl compared her lover to **an apple tree among the trees of the wood**. Flowers and fruit provided the ancient love poets with a rich and wide field of topics from which to select their imagery, as illustrated by Fox's Egyptian love poems. Thus it seems reasonable to assign this **apple tree** to the stock of general rustic imagery used by the ancient erotic poets. Even Pope's casual reference to "the shade of the old apple tree" in the more modern song shows such rustic setting. This is better than detecting here a reference to the apple which, traditionally, Eve gave to Adam at the serpent's bidding in the garden of Eden (Gen. 3:1–7). Eve's apple has had a considerable effect on the interpretation of this verse, as the Heb. words used here for **was in travail**, *ḥibbᵉlaṯkā* and *ḥibbᵉlāh*, both from the same verb, are used sometimes in the Bible of destruction, as indeed earlier in the Song at 2:15, where foxes ruin vineyards. This meaning was detected here by Aquila and Vulg. as indicating Eve's acceptance of the apple in Eden and the consequent corruption of mankind, cf. Vulg.'s *ibi corrupta est mater tua, violata est genetrix tua*, "there was your mother corrupted, she who bore you violated". But the lyric poetry of the Song contains such theological cross-references no more than its earlier Egyptian counterparts. Since the Song is a collection of love poems, a reference to childbirth is not out of place in it; it is better to take that reference at face value than to see it as being full of heavy, symbolic theological meaning. And yet Jews and Christians have often detected such symbolism in the Song, as illustrated in the Afterword.

THE POWER OF LOVE
8:6–7

This short poem of two verses may, as Fox suggests, be a continuation of the second half of v. 5, but the fragmentary nature of that verse (as shown by the gaps between the halves of the verse in *RSV*) makes that doubtful. The themes of vv. 6–7 are different to those of v. 5, anyway: a personal seal, death and the grave, fire and water, riches – these are strong images which describe the fierce vigour of love well and contrast favourably with v. 5's weak echoes of other verses. The **little sister** with **no breasts** of v. 8 is clearly in a different category altogether, and belongs to the next poem. Whereas in vv. 1–5 personal situations were envisaged, here the imagery changes to impersonal forces of some strength: a man's personal **seal** is a possession of considerable authority; **jealousy** (if that is rightly translated – see below) may well be like blazing fire; the destructive power of flooding **waters** is well known. Even **all the wealth** of a man's house (v. 7) seems tame after such strong images.

6. Much may be said about seals. Archaeological excavations in Palestine have uncovered many personal seals from different times. When writing began, seals were used to make official wax impressions on important documents to denote legal authority, cf. "the sealed deed of purchase" regarding Jeremiah's field at Anathoth (Jer. 32:10f.). Tombs were sealed to protect their contents, and seals were placed on jar-handles to show ownership. But seals on signet rings were important not only because of their function but also because of the material from which they were made, for they were often fashioned from precious stones and metals and bore elaborate engravings. Seals were thus among a person's most valuable possessions: in Gen. 38:18 Judah wears his signet on a cord around his neck, guarding it carefully on his person; in Hag. 2:23 the Lord takes Zerubbabel and makes him "like a signet ring" to show that he possesses him and has a special purpose for him. The same comparison with a signet ring is found in the Egyptian love poems: in Fox's poem no. 21C the lover wishes he could be his beloved's precious seal:

> *If only I were her little seal-ring,*
> *the keeper of her finger!*
> *I would see her love* [i.e. her]
> *each and every day.*

Seals were worn either around the neck, dangling **upon your heart**, or as rings on the finger or even further up **your arm**. So here the girl asks her lover to show openly his special relationship with her: she is as precious to him as his own personal seal.

Commentators differ on the exact significance here of *qin'āh*, translated in *RSV* as **jealousy**. *BDB* links the word with deep emotion, giving "ardour, zeal" as well as "jealousy" among the meanings. But there seems little doubt that the bad sense of the word – "jealousy" – occurs much more frequently; the ancient versions agree on that sense here. Indeed, some claim that the word is used only in the pejorative sense. But here there is no third party introduced to provoke **jealousy**, and the parallel line reads, **love is strong as death**; the rest of vv. 6 and 7 deal with **love**, so why should **jealousy** appear? It is unlikely that a contrasting parallelism between these two emotions is intended here; rather, *qin'ah* is probably used here in its less frequent meaning of "passion, ardour". Further, *RSV*'s **cruel** translates the Heb. *qāšāh*, which means "hard, severe" without any emotional connotation. Here it probably describes the compelling power of love – the way in which love, sometimes considered gentle, pushes people in an unrelenting way – as unrelenting as **death** or **the grave**. Gerleman sees the power of love described here by images which gradually intensify: first there is love's strength and relentlessness, and then there is its passionate vehemence, symbolized by **fire** and **floods**. Jealousy doesn't fit such a progression: perhaps a more suitable translation would be "ardour is compulsive", because the power of love is unrelenting **as the grave**.

rĕšĕp̱, here translated **flashes** (**of fire**), is related to the Canaanite god Resheph, who was depicted in iconography as holding weapons. The Heb. noun is used of thunderbolts in Ps. 78:48 and of fiery sparks in Job 5:7. The phrase, **a most vehement flame**, represents an unusual form of the word *šălhĕḇĕṯ*, **flame**: it is intensified with the ending *-yāh*, seemingly an abbreviated form of "Yahweh", the divine name, which is occasionally used to create a superlative expression, since Heb. lacks adjectival forms of the superlative. So the literal meaning here is something like "a God-almighty flame". Similar periphrases for the superlative are seen also in *mă'pēlyāh*, "thickest darkness", in Jer. 2:31 and in *mĕrḥăb-yāh*, "a very spacious place", in Ps. 118:5. It is odd that the only hint of the divine name in the Song should be this curious particle used for the superlative, but this shows how in lyric poetry the divine element was taken into idiomatic usage.

7. This escalating description of the power of love is followed through in v. 7: neither **Many waters** nor even **floods** can **quench** or **drown** love. The phrase, *măyĭm răbbīm*, **Many waters**, occurs twenty-eight times in the OT. Undoubtedly the phrase refers to the insurgent waters of chaos as described in Canaanite and Babylonian myths and echoed in the Bible in passages such as Isa. 51:9, 10 and Ps. 74:10. This topic has been well treated by H. G. May in *JBL* 74 (1955), pp. 9–21; he declared this antithesis between love and many waters to be more penetrating than the simple thought that love is a fire that cannot be put out by water. Rather, it is the powerful floods of the great cosmic deep of ancient mythology that cannot extinguish the power of love. If **Many waters** is to be understood in this mythological way, we can see why it comes as the climax of this poem: the primeval waters were much more threatening than **death** or **fire**.

After this climax, v. 7's last couplet has seemed weak and trivial to some scholars, who have treated it as the insipid, aphoristic comments of a wisdom teacher. However, these words do refer back to the beginning of the poem in v. 6: a personal seal is valuable, but love is more costly than anything money can buy. The couplet may thus be seen as a fitting conclusion to this short poem on the power of love, particularly when we note the forceful use of the Heb. infinitive absolute, *bōz yāḇōzû*, **it would be utterly scorned**, coming at the end.

A DIALOGUE OF PLAYFUL BANTER
8:8–10

These verses clearly belong together as one independent short poem; they are united by the repetition of the words **wall** and **breasts**, and they are distinct from the poem on the power of love in vv. 6 and 7 and from the vineyard theme of vv. 11–12. However, the poem in vv. 8–10 is not easy to interpret. The poet seems to relate a conversation between the girl's brothers, who speak in vv. 8 and 9, and the girl herself, who answers in v. 10. Yet the time-scale seems inconsistent: in v. 8 the girl is described as the brothers' **little sister**, who is too young to have well-formed breasts, yet in v. 10 she replies, or rather retorts, that her breasts are **like towers**: rather a long time apparently passes in a few words. This time-gap may suggest that we are here dealing with memories of the girl's youth, when she was under her brothers' protection. In vv. 8 and 9 the old days of her immaturity are recalled in her brothers' words: they present her as an adolescent who is over-worried about courtship and marriage. They feel they must protect her, and architectural metaphors (**wall**, **battlement**, etc.) are used to express this. But in v. 10 she is suddenly independent: the **little sister** has grown into a sturdy woman, a strong **wall** in her own right with **towers** and no need for **a battlement**. If we are correct in assuming such a time-gap, then the theme of this poem is not unlike that of the previous one – the power of love to bring full maturity to a young woman. But are we correct? Certainly, in prose precise indications of time often appear banal: without them we frequently have to understand the passage of time from the context.

Perhaps this passage can be explained better as the brothers' playful banter. Such light-hearted talk is sometimes found in the Egyptian songs: in Fox's no. 6 (p. 13) the boy feigns sickness to attract his girl's attention, and in no. 7 he thinks up ways to provoke her anger and so make her notice him. Brotherly teasing suits these verses well: the only difficulty is that the apparent climax at the end of v. 10 presents one of the most difficult phrases in the Song to interpret, on any understanding of the previous verses.

8. Usually in the Song the term **sister** is used of the beloved by her lover (cf. 4:9, 10, 12; 5:1, 2) – it is a term of endearment, as in the Egyptian songs. This cannot be its usage here: the beloved has only one lover, who would hardly speak of her as **our sister**, using the first person plural. As there is no hint of rival suitors (*pace* Gordis) – indeed, such rivals would be extremely unlikely to speak of her collectively as their sister! – the speakers here must be the girl's real brothers, not suitors. In the mouths of brothers this tone of authoritarian guardianship is entirely suitable; cf. the role and rights of brothers in Gen. 24:50–55, where Laban negotiates with Abraham's servant for his sister, Rebekah, regarding marriage to Abraham. In Gen. 34:11 similar negotiations are conducted by Dinah's brothers over her marriage to Shechem, and above in ct. 1:6 the girl's **mother's sons were angry** with her because she had not taken care of herself in the fierce sunshine – clear evidence that they felt responsible for her. In the light of the girl's retort in v. 10 the playfulness of the brothers' banter becomes even more apparent. Thus there is no need to postulate a long time-gap: we can well imagine older brothers teasing a kid sister in such a way.

RSV's words, **when she is spoken for** (*šĕyyᵉdŭbbăr-bāh*) are intended to express proposal of marriage: the same phrase (*wăyyᵉdăbbĕr bᵉ-*) is used in 1 Sam. 25:39, where David wooes Abigail to make her his wife.

9. Are walls meant to keep people in or to bar unwanted visitors? As for doors, the very same question may be posed. But whatever defensive, protective significance lies behind the brothers' language here, the fact is that neither **a battlement of silver** nor **boards of cedar** would help in the least to defend the girl's chastity. It may be, as Gerleman suggests, that the primary function of a wall is to hinder entrance and that of a door is to let someone in, but these functions are here secondary to the **silver** and **cedar** decoration. **a battlement of silver** translates *ṭîrăṯ kĕsĕp̱*: in Ezek. 46:23 *ṭîrāh* is used as a synonym for a wall, but the word here appears to denote some superstructure added onto a wall. The emphasis here lies not on the **battlement**'s defensive military function but rather upon the **silver** of which it is made. Similarly, the precise function of the **door** seems irrelevant: its importance here is that its panels are of rich **cedar** (this wood has already been used to imply luxury in 1:17 and 5:15). Cedar decorations were noted as the height of luxury in David's palace (2 Sam. 5:11) and Solomon's temple (1 Kg. 6:10 and *passim*), and in Jer. 22:14f. Jehoiakim's use of cedar panelling in his palace was regarded by the prophet as the epitome of profligate luxury. The girl's brothers are here using such luxurious language to make fun of her defending her virginity.

Goulder sees sheer sexual absurdity in this: "if she is (as flat as) a wall, would it help if they built two turrets on her (chest)?" He notes that three ancient versions (LXX, Vulg., Pesh.) reflect the plural form, "battlements", *ṭîrōṯ* – but singular or plural, the sense is much the same. Goulder continues: "if she is (as flat as) a gate, perhaps they could fix on a reinforcement of cedar boarding in a suitable position?" But how does cedar boarding make her any less flat-chested (which she isn't – see the next verse)? And a gate is a very peculiar image for any chest, flat or curved. The fun which these (typical!) brothers extract from their sister's sexuality isn't as heavy-handed as this: the emphasis lies rather on the luxury of the materials.

10. The girl has the last word in this exchange: she may be a defensive **wall**, but she caps all that teasing nonsense about silver battlements and cedar boards with the bold, provocative statement that her **breasts** are **like towers**. There is, however, one feature of *RSV*'s translation that is puzzling: the girl speaks in the past tense, **I was a wall**, when the Heb. contains no verb to justify that tense until the second part of the verse, **I was in his eyes**, where the perfect is used – presumably to distinguish the phrase from the previous tenseless remarks. Where a sentence has no verb and is purely nominal (as here), the time of the action should be deduced from the context. Here the time reference in vv. 8 and 9 is consistently in the present, with the future used naturally of the brothers' intentions. Therefore, in the absence of any temporal indication, we should take the time from the previous verses, translating, "I am a wall and my breasts are like towers", and then take the perfect, *hayîṯî*, of continuous process in past time: "I have become (in his eyes . . .)".

But the major problem is to describe what she has become: *RSV* has **as one who brings peace**, cf. *NEB*. In the Heb. (*k*ᵉ*môṣ'ēṯ šālōm*) the participle *k*ᵉ*môṣ' eṯ* raises several problems. The preposition *k*ᵉ need not worry us: often used as a particle of comparison ("as", "like"), it can also denote a certain assuring emphasis ("surely") as the *kaph veritatis* described in *G-K* § 118x. Thus this particle may give a certain weight and emphasis to the culminating phrase of this short section which is hardly translatable in English: "verily" or "indeed" would make too much of it. It is unfortunately not clear which verb the participle *môṣ' ēṯ* comes from: it could be the contracted (cf. *G-K* § 74i) Qal participle feminine singular of *māṣā'*, "found" (whence *RSV* margin: "as one who finds peace"), or the Hiphil participle feminine singular of *yāṣā'*, "went out", meaning here "bringing out, offering" (whence *RSV* text: **as one who brings peace**, cf. *NEB*). The noun *šālōm* may be used of terms for peace as in, for example, Dt. 20:10 (*w*ᵉ*qārāṯā 'ēlĕyhā l*ᵉ*šālōm* – "(then) offer terms of peace to it (the city)") and Jg. 21:13 (*wayyiqr*ᵉ*'û lāhĕm šālōm* – "and they proclaimed peace to them"). *NEB* speaks of "one who brings contentment", presumably thinking of a love scene; so too *JB* which has "under his eyes I have found true peace". But the context of this short poem is not that of a courting couple but rather that of brothers using military metaphors to tease their sister. Goulder, citing Dt. 20:10, writes: "when a city is surrendering, a delegation must come out, offering and suing for peace". In the eyes of her lover the girl is making peace in the family: the military metaphor is continued and concluded as she climbs down from her proud position and **brings peace** to her brothers.

TWO DIFFERENT VINEYARDS
8:11–12

In 6:8f. the beloved was compared favourably with the women of Solomon's royal harem; here in this short poem she is described as a **vineyard** and is compared with Solomon's **vineyard at Baal-hamon**. The vineyard theme has appeared before in 1:6, 2:15 and 4:12–14. In 1:6 the girl was accused of not keeping her own vineyard, whereas here (v. 12) her vineyard is for herself alone, and she is quite content with it. The fact that verses near the beginning of the Song and others near the end of it share a similar theme gives substance to Shea's views on chiastic structure (*ZAW* 92 (1980), pp. 378–96), and suggests that the collection of these poems was not as random as some suggest (see Introduction). The fruits of the orchard in 4:12–14 are sealed off, locked away from marauders; similarly, in 2:15 the blossoms of **our vineyards** are in danger from the attacks of little foxes. Here such danger of pillage is absent: the beloved's vineyard is for no-one else, and its value is beyond all price. This short poem thus serves as a culmination of the other three passages.

11. Fox draws attention to the construction of the first few words in the Heb.: *kerem hāyāh lisᵉlōmōh bᵉḇaʿal hāmōn*, **Solomon had a vineyard at Baal-hamon**. This he claims to be a regular opening for a parable, comparing Isa. 5:1: *kerem hāyāh lîḏîḏî*, "my beloved had a vineyard". Parable or not, we should ask if the vineyard referred to is a real one: in Jdt. 8:3 there is mention of a place called Balamon (a reasonable English transliteration of the Greek equivalent of the Heb. name here). Said to be near Dothan, this place is thought by Gordis to be possibly Tel Balame, 2 km. south of Jenin. It is quite possible that the author of 8:11–12 chose a real vineyard which was reputed to have actually belonged to Solomon – that wealthy king would have owned many vineyards, perhaps including one whose name happened to fit symbolically the present context. **Baal-hamon** means "possessor of wealth"; the word *hāmōn* can refer to a multitude of people or richness in money and possessions, and thus it could fit Solomon's legendary wealth well. Goulder's nickname for Solomon, "own-a-lot", brings out the word-play well.

But whether the vineyard is a real location or not, its symbolic meaning has real significance here, contrasted with **my very own** vineyard in the next verse. It is unnecessary with Rudolph to see here a veiled reference to Jerusalem: the word-play in the subject-matter is sufficient justification for using *Baathamon* – particularly in the light of the next verse, which makes plain the contrast between Solomon's financial wealth and the lover's treasure in his beloved, which is far more valuable than all Solomon's hoard. Further, Solomon leased his vineyard out to tenants, but the speaker here has her lover all to herself (cf. the tremendously emphatic construction of *karmî sellî lᵉp̱ānăy* – **My vineyard, my very own, is for myself** in the next verse).

a thousand pieces of silver: as often in the OT, the unit of measurement is missing in the Heb. (cf. Gen. 20:16, for example): the Heb. here reads literally, "a thousand of silver", leaving the actual unit of currency to be understood. We should probably understand "shekels", although most English translations join *RSV* in inserting the vague word **pieces**. In Isa. 7:23 land worth "a thousand shekels of silver" is regarded as very valuable. The **thousand pieces of silver** here would be received by the tenant for the fruit he had tended. He would keep **two hundred** pieces for himself (as stated in the next verse), passing the rest on to his landlord.

12. The **vineyard** metaphor is here used in reverse: the girl has previously been described as her lover's garden (1:6, 4:16), but here she says most emphatically, **My vineyard, my very own, is for myself**, meaning either her own sexual charms or, more probably, her lover. The general sense is clear: Solomon has plenty of vineyards (i.e. plenty of girls in his harem), and each of them brings him a profit of **a thousand pieces of silver**, although the business arrangement seems to allow a cut of **two hundred** for **the keepers of the fruit**, i.e. the tenants who actually grow the fruit for the distant royal landlord. Solomon's vineyard represents his large harem; but this simple image has grown in the description, taking on further details irrelevant to the main point. The numbers are included to contrast *the thousand* with *my very own.* As Fox remarks, "the specification of the keeper's wages seems superfluous". Yes, the metaphor has certainly grown a bit, though it could be argued that oversight of large numbers – of vineyards or of women in a harem – could lead to preoccupation with administration of the household rather than caring loyalty in relationships.

But such problems of size are happily far from the girl's situation; her **vineyard** (the term now used of the man or of her love relationship) is her own private matter: it is *l^ep̄ānăy*, **for myself** (a phrase used in Prov. 4:3, where the (male) child is the only one *lĭp̄^enēy*, "in the sight of (his mother)"). So here the beloved is in control of her own life, not subject to the conventions of a court harem. Human love is more direct than that: the girl and her lover enjoy a free and exclusive relationship.

A CLOSING INVITATION
8:13–14

This may seem a strange heading to give to the last two verses, but they form a very odd conclusion to the Song! Whether the Song is one complete composition or a collection of individual love songs, we might expect some climax, some conclusion – and yet here we seem to have just more of the same. This has prompted some scholars to suggest that the original ending has been lost and that we have here only fragments of another poem. Yet v. 14 seems to echo earlier material, with phrases from 2:17. As we noted above on 8:5, some of this last chapter seems fragmentary, and the arrangement of the text in *RSV* supports this view by leaving large gaps between the verses here. There is no textual evidence to suggest that once the Song contained more material than it does now, so we must make the best of what we have, assuming that these verses have always been at the end.

Lys and Fox suggest that the Song never reaches completion, just like love, which is never satisfied: true love is always a quest, a going on, a looking forward. Certainly, the Song never completely fulfils the desires of the two lovers in any formal marriage: v. 14 here seems to sum up the whole experience of the lovers with each other, using quotations from earlier passages to do it. So, since there is no recognized stage or goal in the lovers' relationship to be reached, and as all loving relationships are ongoing and look towards the future, it seems fitting to leave the lovers doing just that!

13. This verse is addressed to the girl: the feminine participle, **you who dwell**, the feminine suffix on **your voice** and the feminine singular imperative, **let me hear**, all make this plain. The speaker is thus the young man. On the plural form of **gardens**, see the commentary on the similar use in 6:2. That young people should dally **in the gardens** seems to fit the Egyptian background: love in the garden is discussed as a major theme by Fox on pp. 283–7, and in the Egyptian songs collected by him there are many references to gardens, meadows, fields and the like, as indeed in the Song itself (cf. 4:12f., 6:2, 11). The young man's **companions** here may be rivals for the girl's affection, as Gerleman suggests; but is it not likely that the young men in those days would have hung around girls in ancient Egypt, just as they do today? But if he and his companions are sitting, waiting for her **voice**, it is strange if we do not hear it! The next verse is addressed by the girl to her lover – the gender of the verbs and nominal suffixes again makes this plain. If Gerleman is right in thinking that v. 14 is the girl's response to the lover's words in v. 13, then we should really enclose v. 14 in inverted commas as citing the girl's actual words in response.

14. The close likeness of this verse to 2:17 has already been noted in the introduction to this section: it is the differences between the two verses which perhaps need special comment here. Whereas 2:17 reads, **turn, my beloved**, here we have,

Make haste, my beloved – a translation which tries to make sense of the Heb. word *b^{e}răḥ*, a verb which normally means "flee" – but who is there to flee from here? Different English translations do their best with "come into the open" (*NEB*), "haste away" (*JB* – possibly the neatest) and "bolt away" (Fox). The addition of "away" may bring the translation nearer to the normal meaning of *b^{e}răḥ*, but it raises the question even more pointedly: "bolt away" from what and from whom? Even if we accept that the basic meaning of *b^{e}răḥ* is "to proceed speedily" (which is doubtful) and thus see the lovers happily hastening to be with each other, the predominant meaning of fleeing as proceeding speedily *from* some place leaves us perplexed. We should also note Gerleman's disquiet that the lover, after asking to hear his beloved's voice, is then exhorted to flee away in terms reminiscent of young love: and where is the expected invitation to take his beloved with him? Pesh. lightens the verbal idea by translating "turn", but this is only reading the same text as in the parallel passage in 2:17, and the different word is attested here by LXX and Vulg. But perhaps it is depending too much on modern ideas of love to expect the two to flee away together. It is more likely that we have here another play on words: although the noun *b^{e}rīăḥ* was not used for the **bolt** of 5:5, it is a natural word for a "bolt" if *bārīăḥ*, "a bolt", is used here with the second sense adopted in the commentary on 5:5, thus suggesting the *double entendre* implied here. Could the verb here indicate at the same time both the lover's departure from the companions of v. 13 and his sexual approaches to his beloved – another case of *double entendre*? That would explain the mention of the **gazelle** and the **young stag** in this verse: as Pope points out, these animals' names are used in Mesopotamian incantations to heal sexual impotence: the stag in particular is used in this way.

the mountains of spices (*hārē b^{e}sāmîm*) replace the **rugged mountains** of 2:17; although Pesh. reads the same in both places, LXX and Vulg. show knowledge of a different text. In 4:6 the lover said that he would go **to the mountain of myrrh and the hill of frankincense**: spices and smells like this occur frequently enough in the Egyptian lyrics for us to accept them as part of the background of the Song.

So the Song closes with the lovers making haste to go off on their own amid all the erotic fauna and flora of oriental love poetry.

AFTERWORD

Something has already been said in the Introduction about the ways in which Jewish and Christian scholars have interpreted the Song by allegory and symbolism. The purpose behind this commentary has been to expound the Song's natural meaning against contemporary setting and tradition, without allowing that natural meaning to be smothered by later Jewish and Christian accretions. Readers wishing to study such interpretations through the centuries should consult the commentaries of Robert/Tournay/Feuillet and Pope, where these matters receive detailed attention – Pope even gives a translation of the Targum. However, it seems right after expounding the natural meaning to note some of the ways in which the Song has been handled in the past: so, rather than giving a full, and perhaps tedious, account of trends, I have chosen to concentrate on several passages as illustrations.

One passage that seems to pious commentators in need of spiritual interpretation is that of the **banqueting house** of 2:4. Those who see in the Song a celebration of human marriage (in fact marriage is never mentioned) see here a wedding feast. Those who read the Song in the context of Near-Eastern fertility rites detect here a reference to sacred prostitution. The Jewish Targum made the **banqueting house** the academy of research on Sinai – a fanciful way of indicating the sustaining and refreshing power that lay in the study of the Law. The Midrash Rabbah tamely gave way to computing the numerical value of the Hebrew letters used for **and his banner** (*wdglw*): the resulting total, 49, was held to refer to the number of reasons for declaring something clean or unclean. Some Christian scholars followed hints from Jerome in the Vulgate, where the Latin *ordinavit* is used, and saw here a reference to admission into the Catholic Church, where alone the wine of the Spirit could be reliably found. The **banqueting house** has, then, been explained as God's altar, where the wine of salvation is received in the Eucharist. Others have seen here a reference to the Incarnation, in which Jesus' body housed the divine Word which was the true wine of the soul.

What, then, one asks, have people done with the **litter of Solomon** and its **sixty mighty men** in 3:7? For the Targum Solomon's litter is the temple which he built and furnished so richly (cf. 3:9, 10), and the **sixty mighty men** are the priests spreading their hands over the congregation, pronouncing the 60 letters of the priestly blessing. The Midrash Rabbah accepts this interpretation, but suggests that the number may also represent the divisions of priests and Levites (24 + 24) plus the people of Israel (12 tribes). Some Christians have seen Solomon's bed as the Church, where saints delight to embrace the true lover of their souls. Various computations of the number 60 have been offered: David's élite guard, for example, numbered 30, but his kingdom was only the Jewish community; the new Solomon (Christ) rules both Jews and Christians, whence the number is doubled (30 + 30 = 60).

The *waṣfs* lend themselves naturally to allegorical interpretation, with their orderly sequences of bodily parts. Thus the Targum sees the girl's teeth (4:2) as referring to the priests and Levites who ate the temple sacrifices, and her lips (4:3) are the lips of the high priest saying prayers on the Day of Atonement. The scarlet colour of her lips reminded some Christians of the blood shed by Christ at his passion, though others, oddly, have detected here the scarlet thread which Rahab the harlot placed in her window at Jericho to save her life (Josh. 2:18, 21). The Targum reads **the tower of David** (4:4) (which is not a real building) as a reference to the principal of the rabbinic academy; Christians have interpreted it as meaning the heads of the Church. And what of the girl's breasts (v. 5)? The Targum relates these to two Messiahs (one descended from David and one from Ephraim), or alternatively to Moses and Aaron; Christian interpreters introduce the two Testaments, or love of God and love of neighbour, etc.

In view of all this, it comes as no surprise that the sexier aspects of the girl's dream in 5:2–8 are played down considerably or even ignored. The girl's heart staying awake while she sleeps (v. 2) is identified by the Targum with Israel's sin and punishment in exile, followed by her return home. The Midrash Rabbah saw in the girl's sleep Israel's ambivalent attitude to religious practice, and Christians have detected in it the relaxation of zeal following the end of persecution. The man's hair being **wet with dew** represents God's hair being soaked by the tears of his people. The girl's removal of her **garment** in v. 3 meant for the Targum the removal of the yoke of the Law in order to worship idols, but in the Midrash Rabbah this indicated Nebuchadnezzar stripping the king and the priests of their vestments when he destroyed Jerusalem. The **hand** of v. 4 is, of course, not seen sexually: in the Targum it signifies God's blow against the northern kingdom when he gave it to the Assyrians. Christians seem to have interpreted it of God's hand weakened as through a keyhole.

The interpretations which have been brought to the Song to make it religious have been many and varied, as these few examples show. For this reason it seems better to take the Song as a celebration of God-given human love, as we have done in this commentary.

GENERAL INDEX

INDEX OF AUTHORS